What They're Saying About Kathy Hill

It's a blessing to see the content that is being shared in these 15 dynamic principles. Success and prosperity are very important for the Kingdom of God. Kathy does an astounding job in explaining her testimony and her success. May this book bless you and everyone you purchase one for. Let it be a blessing!

> Dr. Phillip G. Goudeaux
> Sr. Pastor Calvary Christian Center
> Sacramento, CA

I am excited to see committed Christ followers like Kathy Hill of TAX TIGER recognizing that they are Kingdom ambassadors in the marketplace. Join Kathy in making sure your business has God's hand on it.

> Dr. John Jackson
> President of William Jessup University

Kathy Hill is committed to Christ's righteousness inside of her business practices. Her examples of how God can lead ordinary people into extraordinary results by placing His amazing, sovereign and purposefully hand on your business will both inspire you as well as demonstrate a road for you to follow.

> Eric Hogue, Chief Develo⌐
> William Jessup University

This is a wonderful book, full of guida⌐ help you to take God as your partner, and ⌐ to Him. When you do, you will never make another mistake.

> Brian Tracy
> Author, *Million Dollar Habits*

I have had a front row seat to the unfolding story of success in the life of Kathy Hill. The principles she teaches are those that she lives by. It is those very principles which have propelled her to the top of her field—the same principles that are transferable and will fuel success for anyone who will embrace them and put them into practice. As I read this book, I found inspiration and tools for my own personal growth. You will want to read this more than once and mark the pages for easy reference. Then, you will want to provide a copy for the people in your life that you love and care about. It is that good!!

> Rick J. Cole
> Pastor, Capital Christian Center
> Sacramento, Ca

Faith does precede the Miracle. This books tells the reader that hope does exist and gives him the faith to trust in God.

> Kirby Cochran
> Professor of Finance, Author
> and Businessman

If you are looking for the success path to follow to experience an increased level of success in your personal life and in your business, I highly recommend this gem. Success is your birthright. Create it in your life starting today.

> Peggy McColl
> *New York Times* Best-Selling Author

Is God's Hand On Your Business?

Is God's Hand On Your Business?

15 Essential Principles for Success and Prosperity

Kathy Hill

Founder and CEO
Tax Tiger, Inc.

Is God's Hand On Your Business?
15 Essential Principles for Success and Prosperity
By Kathy Hill

Books may be purchased by contacting the publisher and author at:
kathyhill@kathyhillauthor.com

Cover and Interior Design: Nick Zelinger (NZ Graphics)
Publisher: Rainbow Press Books
Editor: John Maling (Editing By John)
Manuscript and Book Consultant: Judith Briles (The Book Shepherd)

ISBN: 978-0-9893278-0-0 (print)

ISBN: 978-0-9893278-1-7 (e-book)

Library of Congress Control Number: 2013907200

1) Business Memoir   2) Christian Faith   3) Tax Liability

First Edition

Printed in the USA

To my Heavenly Father, whose hand continues
To hover over my business

To my sons, David and John Paul
Who continue to make me proud

And to my Dad, who "taught me
In the way I should go"

Table of Contents

Foreword

When the Lord laid it on my heart to start Tax Tiger, I felt like Moses in the Old Testament. You remember the story—how God called him to be the leader of the Jewish people who were in slavery, and led them out of Egypt and across the desert to the Promised Land.

If you don't remember, you can find it in Exodus 3. It went something like this: Moses was a simple shepherd walking through the hills as he had always done, tending his sheep, when he came upon something astonishing. Before him was a bush burning, yet it failed to be consumed. He turned aside to see this strange happening and when he did, God spoke from the bush, directly to him:

> Moses, I have seen the misery of my people in Egypt. I have heard them crying out against their slave masters; and I am concerned about their suffering. Therefore, go to them; I am sending you to bring my people out of Egypt.

Moses said, (my own words) "Who, me? Why me? I am not eloquent of speech, I stutter, and I am not worthy of this appointment to lead your people."

God replied, "Who made your mouth? ... *Now go, and I* **will go with you**, *I will be with you, I will help you speak and will teach you what to say.*"

When my husband, Dick, suggested to me that I start a tax resolution company, it was a "burning bush moment" for me. I was a simple sales rep who used to sell Tupperware in my early years.

In my heart, I said, "Who, me? I am inadequate for this leadership role; I don't have a college degree in business, or experience in running a corporation, nor do I have the proper credentials to negotiate with the IRS. It was an overwhelming idea ..."

But it was also one which God implanted in my heart and then said, "*I will go with you and show you what to say and do.*"

I have relied on God's hand on my business from day one, because I knew I could never do it just with my own skill and ability ... And God held true to His promise to me as He did to Moses. He has walked with me daily through this exciting journey to lead taxpayers who are suffering out from under the oppression of the IRS—people originally with no hope of a solution to their problems. These people I help suffer from extreme financial hardships with wage and bank levies and don't yet understand how to get to the "promised land" of financial freedom.

It has not been an easy road, but one filled with gratitude and joy over the amazing number of people who have been lead "out of Egypt"—from the oppression of the IRS—and have seen their IRS debt disappear before their eyes. And it's all because I was obedient in the things He asked of me and the things I did on a daily basis that had His hand over my business, leading me to the kind of success I would never have dreamed of otherwise. These secrets of my success will be revealed in *Is God's Hand On Your Business?* and I encourage you to make them your own.

To make a difference in people's lives is my motto, and it has been—and still is—unbelievably rewarding.

This is my calling, and to God goes **all the honor and glory.**

Kathy

For I know the plans I have for you, declares the Lord,
plans to prosper you and not to harm you;
plans to give you hope and a future.
–Jeremiah 29:11 NIV

If the Lord delights in a man's way, he makes his
steps firm; though he stumble, he will not fall,
for the Lord upholds him with His hand.
–Psalm 37:23 and 24

1

My Childhood Was My Roots

Born and raised into a Pastor's family, I was known as a "PK"—a preacher's kid—since I was five years old. My Dad pastored a Baptist church in Colorado, where I grew up. Life for me then was constantly listening to sermons, meeting wonderful visiting missionaries who stayed with us in our home, and learning, knowing and loving the Bible stories of the Old Testament.

Christ wasn't always my personal savior, as He is now. I'm not sure why it took me so long, since I sat listening to my Dad's preaching three to four times a week, year after year. All I can say is that God has a plan, and there is a time for everything. It just wasn't in His will for me when I was a kid. That changed, however, when I was twelve.

I felt an immediate peace and I now knew where I would go if I died.

One night, after the Sunday evening service was over and I was getting ready for bed, God spoke to me. I remember lying there in bed, in the dark, and hearing the Lord speak to me through my thoughts. He asked me just one simple question,

"If you died tonight, where would you go?" I was shocked and scared because I knew it was God speaking to me, and I could feel the conviction in my heart—I knew the answer and it scared me. I would go to hell. I had not accepted Christ into my heart nor asked for forgiveness of my sins, even after hearing the plan of salvation all those many years.

As I lay there in the dark, I bowed my head on the pillow and asked Jesus to come into my heart and forgive my sins. I felt an immediate peace, and I now knew where I would go if I died. I had a home in heaven with my name on it, and little did I know that God had a plan for my life—one I had no idea of, nor would I have ever believed possible.

Being the daughter of a pastor, God was never far away—His hand touched my life in many different ways. One memory of mine is a story my Dad tells about me—I don't remember it happening but Dad assures me that it had and I was the genesis. It is impressive in demonstrating the way God uses people in unique and special ways.

I was only five, and this incident happened one Sunday morning before service. We were praying the blessing over breakfast and I was asked to say the prayer. I prayed for the Lord to "save" my Sunday school teacher, Mrs. Wilson. After the prayer was over, my father expressed astonishment. He said to me, "Kathy, your teacher, Mrs. Wilson, is already a Christian, and so you don't need to pray for her to be saved." I replied emphatically, "No, Daddy, she is not and she needs to be saved."

He thought it was just the imagination of a child and let it go. But lo and behold, after the morning service, Mrs.

Wilson came down the aisle, with tears streaming down her face. She said, "Pastor, all these years I thought I was a Christian, but I realized today that I had never actually confessed my sin and asked Jesus to come into my heart and life. I need to do that today."

My Dad was flabbergasted. He had led her to the Lord and had assumed she fully had insured her place with God. He was amazed at how God used a little child to pray for something he thought he knew and she didn't even understand. God uses children in mighty ways.

Faithfulness

Another story that stands out clearly, even after all these years, happened in my junior year of high school. It is a lesson I learned in being faithful to God and his teachings, no matter what. It was a hard lesson for a teenager to learn, but it is one I learned and will never forget.

A beauty pageant was to be held at the State Fair coming up in a few months. Hundreds of girls were going to try out. The brochure circulated through the school and our church. I wanted to try out but didn't believe I had a chance in the world of winning anything. Never the less my tender, teenage heart overcame my head and wished it could be so. There were 20 girls who would win a spot on the 20 floats, and I wanted to win one of those spots badly. To ride on the back of a convertible wearing a Miss _____ Something ribbon would have been a dream come true for this teenage girl— me.

I asked permission from my mother, and she said "Yes." Having a nice dress to try out in was a major problem, because we didn't have much money. My Mom was an excellent seamstress and said she would make me one. I therefore put in my application and was given a two minute speech to memorize and recite from memory in front of a panel of judges. The tryouts would be held at a large hotel in town at a certain date and time. But oh no!!! The date fell on a Wednesday evening—a church night. When I asked my Dad if I could miss that one Wednesday evening Bible study, he said—emphatically—"No!"

I was told in no uncertain terms that one doesn't miss church for any reason other than being sick and unable to attend. He said God would not bless me if I was to miss church, and, besides, I probably wouldn't win anyway. I pleaded, and cried, and he still said no. My mother tried to intercede, but it was still, no! My Dad always practiced what he preached. Being faithful to God was an absolute with him.

So, I tried to think of ways around it. Even at that young age, I could bring to bear certain creative skills with which I had been blessed. The plan I came up with offered the solution to the problem "eating my cake and having it too." That is, of attending service that evening and still making the pageant tryouts. The tryouts started at 7:00 pm and would go on for an hour and possibly more as each girl gave her speech before the judges. I called the organizer, explained my situation and asked if it were possible for me to come late and be the last to speak. I figured then I just might have enough time to get there after service if I hurried like crazy.

My Mom agreed to drive me there right after church, and my Dad reluctantly agreed to let me go. I worked on memorizing my two-minute speech and Mom made me a dress. On the big night, I went to church dressed as nicely as I could make myself, ready to bolt out the door when the service was over despite the fact my Dad believed it was an exercise in futility because he knew I would not make it. I prayed for days for God to help me, and, once out of the church, I continued to pray as my Mom raced me toward the hotel and the try-out. I had been faithful; I had gone to church and put God first. Now, would He come through for me?

It took us longer to get there than I had planned and I literally ran for the auditorium. There were hundreds of people sitting there and to my horror, the last girl had finished and the panel of seven judges had already gone to a private room to begin deliberations. I was too late. But what happened next is what I call "a God story." I will never forget how God interceded for me that evening as long as I live.

The woman in charge knew I was to be placed last and had been watching for me to show up. When I got there too late and she saw my crestfallen face, she made an unusual and split-second decision. She said the judges had already begun their deliberations but she was going to go ask them if they would hear one last girl.

Unbelievably, they said yes. She led me down a long hallway to their room, and I entered a room occupied by the judges. I was confronted with seven stern-faced men all looking at me. I was now terrified and didn't even know if I could remember my words. One kind man lost his stern look, smiled and told me to go ahead. Just as I started, the wind blew a window behind them shut, making a loud noise. It startled me and I stopped talking and lost my place.

I knew I wasn't the prettiest girl but every girl has a dream ...

I thought I was done and it was all over. I was convinced I had gotten this far only to fail. Instead, they all smiled and said, "It's OK young lady, just start over again." I did, and managed to get through my whole speech.

I thanked them and retreated to the auditorium where my Mom waited as did one of my best friends from church. Let me explain here that my best friend also had filled out an application but her parents didn't make her attend service that evening. They believed that sometimes things other than sickness did happen to prevent church attendance, but as long as you continued to go on a regular basis, it was OK.

She was prettier than I was and so were many of the other girls trying out. I knew I wasn't anywhere near the prettiest girl even, but every girl has a dream of winning a beauty pageant, and I was handing my dream over to God. I knew He had the power to make anything happen. I knew a miracle had just happened by being allowed to compete after the speeches had officially closed. I had peace in my heart, but not a conviction that I would win. It was more than very doubtful.

The results were in. We all waited anxiously as they began to call the names. With over 200 applicants, spots started to fill. They called name after name and none of them were mine. It was now down to the very last name ... AND IT WAS MINE! The tears streamed down my face as I walked to the front. I was named Miss Legal Aid Society, and they placed the banner around me. God came through for me. He didn't have to; it wasn't a huge deal in the big picture of spiritual things, but I learned that evening that He cares about our longings and dreams no matter how small.

When we got home, I raced into the house shouting to my Dad, "I won, I won!" He was very surprised, but told me I won because I had honored God first and was faithful. Even though I was forced into it, I learned a lesson that night on faithfulness that I have never forgotten, and, to this day, I don't miss church service on Sunday unless I'm sick and simply unable to get there.

When I went to thank the judges afterward, they told me that there was something about me that stood out to them. To this day, I believe that it was God shining through me in some small way. Not surprisingly, my girlfriend was very upset—she couldn't see how I could have won coming late as I had. I told her she should have gone to church like I did and maybe God would have blessed her too. My heart was over-flowing with thanksgiving to God for an answered prayer and the granting of a young girls dream.

That experience was my first and most powerful lesson on both answered prayer and faithfulness—I'll never forget it as long as I live. Having faith ... Believing ... God was preparing me for much more, and His hand was on my life, ready to steer and direct me.

2

It All Started with Tupperware

My story of business success started with a financial need. How often can you say there was a financial need in your life? Probably more times than you'd like to admit. Fast forward a few years. I am now married and a young stay-at-home mom with two little boys, ages seven and three. Being a stay-at-home mom was a decision that I made by choice.

Before my boys were born, my husband, Marty, and I had attended a parenting seminar given by a top psychologist in Dallas, Texas. He taught that it was crucial for a mother to remain at home with her children, if at all possible, until they went to school. The reasoning for this was that children need the security of her presence for healthy emotional development during their early formative years.

Since we both agreed this was vitally important for the emotional stability of our children, we decided that I would not work until they both were in school. Financially, this can be a hard decision if there is only one income in the family— and I'm sure it's harder today than it was 30 years ago. Marty had a good paying job with the post office, so this worked for us. His income was enough to pay all the basic bills, but not enough for any extras. We were living in a duplex but really wanted to have our own home. We found a beautiful, brand new, two story home in a new development, perfect for us now that we had two little boys. This was back in the days when homes were both more affordable and interest rates were low.

After a lot of calculating, we figured we could just barely make the mortgage and the basic bills. Our loan was approved, and we were incredibly excited to have a brand new house for our family. This home had no landscaping; there was just dirt in the front and back yards. Fortunately, I was blessed with a husband who was extremely mechanically inclined and could build, fix or design just about anything. A lot of money can be saved when you can do it yourself, and that was the case with us. He did a lot of our handyman work and did it as well if not better than any professional.

Having all the furniture we needed, we squeezed out enough money for paint and wallpaper, and into the front and back yard dirt went grass seed, once up, creating a luscious green carpet around the house. Problem: My big issue was drapes. Other families were moving into the neighborhood and in each occupied house—now a home— the windows were lined with newspapers for curtains!

Ugh—I was appalled. I'm very big on neatness and color coordination and can't stand to live in a home without some visual attractiveness. I determined in my heart there would be no newspapers on our windows. I honestly don't think this was a pride issue as much as it grated on my sense of orderliness and offended my design talents.

Shopping was next, but when I started to price drapes, I got a huge shock. It was to be either cheap, off-the-rack curtains, or beautiful custom drapes which would make the windows elegant. Keep in mind that sometimes God gives us the desires of our hearts ... and sometimes he doesn't. I believe in praying for everything, big or small, a need or just a want. I leave the answer to Him and am always grateful either way He answers.

My "cause" became the window coverings, and I admit, I like pretty things—Marty could have cared less what was on the windows. The custom drapes I had priced from JC Penney's came to $2,000 to cover all the windows in the house—that was a lot of money. When I talked to my husband about it, all he said was, "No way. The cheap, off-the-rack ones are just fine."

I now had a clear financial need, and no idea on how to get any extra money to cover my $2,000 "necessity." Until I found the money, my windows would have nothing but clear glass.

Be Willing to Learn New Things

Right here is where God's hand became evident in the plan for my overall business success—something that would take years to achieve but, to my delight, the first step began here with my problem with the curtains. And I can look back on my life and see the progression of steps that God had ordered for me according to His word. I made mistakes along the way, but my steps were still ordered. He forgives our mistakes, loves us in spite of them and blesses our efforts.

*I had never sold anything in my life,
but selling was required, and this was
a totally off-the-wall idea.*

One evening, I had an invitation to attend a Tupperware party from a girlfriend at our church. Not needing any myself, I went out of obligation to her as well as to have a night out with friends. The presenter's name was Monica. She had a very outgoing, personable demeanor and did a great job making the evening enjoyable. And, along the way, she sold a good number of Tupperware bowls. At the end of the evening, she made an offer to anyone needing additional income to consider becoming a "Tupperware lady." What got my attention quickly was when she said, "The money was good for a part-time job of just a few hours a week—Tupperware was looking for more women to be reps."

I sat there and listened. Bingo, the light bulb went off. I wondered in my heart if this was something I could do. The more I thought about it, the more it seemed like the solution to the financial need for the drapes. Now, keep in mind I had never sold anything in my life and this was a totally off-the-wall idea. But the idea took root and I believe that when God puts a plan before you, He will provide the way. There is a quote I've heard and love:

Where God guides, God provides.

I would experience this many times over the next years of my life.

I also believe that you need to be willing to learn new things as He brings them your way. This was something I would have to learn to do. I had never stood up in front of women and tried to sell anything. But, how hard could it be? The Tupperware bowls were great bowls, made of superior quality material, and women loved them. I was willing to learn. *Where God guides, God provides* kept running through my head.

My mind was in high gear. *God has given talents to his children. He expects us to use them. He orders our steps. He has a plan for us; there are blessings and favor waiting to be given.* Then came the clincher—the Tupperware lady got my attention again. She said, "I'm a manager and all managers get a brand new car, right from the factory, every two years."

We only had one car and here was the solution to get another—with two little boys, having my own car would truly be a blessing. I asked, "What had to be done to earn a car?"

"Just recruit five new Tupperware ladies after you start doing your own parties," was her immediate response.

I had never recruited anyone for anything, but how hard could that be?

I went home that night so excited and full of enthusiasm to explain to my husband how I was going to get us custom drapes—all at the same time! I got the manager's phone number and couldn't wait to talk to my husband. As soon as I got in the door, I started telling him about my idea and the plan that would give us additional income for all the extras we needed. All I asked was that he watch the kids for a couple of hours in the evening for two or three evenings a week. That week. That would allow me to be at home during the day with them and still earn the extra income we could use.

As I started to explain my plan, he stopped me with one word, "No."

I stared at him dumbfounded. "What do you mean, No? You haven't even heard me out. And I can get us a new car!"

He said, "No company gives away a new car just for recruiting five women into the company; I don't believe it." I was so angry that I had not been given the courtesy of a discussion nor of even being allowed to complete my thoughts or finish speaking. It was just a flat out No. End of discussion.

Anyone who knows me well knows that was the wrong thing to say to me. So after a minute or two, I said, "I'm calling the lady first thing in the morning and I'm signing up." Now it was the end of discussion.

I can't claim to be proud of being disobedient and lacking in submission, but no one is perfect! I figured I would answer for not being in submission but he would also answer for being rude, disrespectful, and ridiculing my idea. In hindsight, maybe I could have found another way to help him see the light, but my anger took over and there was no further discussion.

The next morning, I called Monica and told her I wanted to sign up immediately. She came over, we filled out the paperwork and I was given some training. I got a Tupperware kit to demonstrate from, and all I needed to do then was to find women to have parties for me. This was the hardest part. But once I got going, more and more parties were booked. I made a huge effort to be creative and make my parties fun and entertaining, so I created games and there was always fun and laughter. I discovered, much to my surprise, that I was good at it.

The talent that God had given me blossomed and grew weekly. I loved being up in front of the ladies and I got better and better at it. It only took me six weeks to recruit my five into the business. My car was straight from Detroit. It really was just that simple and there were no other strings attached.

It was a beautiful station wagon. The day it came in, I drove it home, parked in the driveway and watched my husband hang his head. I do believe a little gloating was in order. Remember, he told me it would never happen and I could never do it. It was the most wonderful feeling of achievement and God's favor. I was very proud of what I had accomplished.

Gratitude and Attitude

With each party that I delivered, I never knew if I would earn a little money or a significant amount—or a lot. God taught me through them, that I was to trust Him and be grateful for whatever I got, be it a little "or a lot." When I had a party that brought in hundreds of dollars in sales, I would thank and praise Him. With those times when I sold only a few dollars and made nothing for my time, I learned what it meant to be grateful, and to praise Him for the little He gave me. I verbally stated this belief to my group of ladies I had recruited and it began to be a testimony for my faith.

Initially discouraged with minimal sales, I learned how God is still in there directing steps. Even when your heart is in the right place and you have a positive attitude, the failures can be disappointing and sometimes disconcerting. Having absolute faith and trust, no matter what happens, is the key to His magic kingdom. God promises to guide and direct our steps. He has also given to each person talent and abilities that ar: unique. Discovering what those talents are can be a journey fraught with road bumps and trial and error. Up to this time, I never knew I had sales capability, or people skills, or leadership ability. I learned this over time by trusting that God knew best, and by being willing to learn something new. I felt God had become my business partner.

I learned what it meant to be grateful, and to praise Him for the little He gave me.

I sold Tupperware for approximately 10 years and became one of the top Tupperware ladies in California, earning many gifts and awards on top of the additional income brought to my family. Oh, and lest I forget, I had earned the $2,000 for the custom drapes in less than 90 days, selling one burping bowl at a time! I never put one newspaper on my windows—God is so good!

Transitions

God had a business transition in store for me. Transitions are never easy in life or in business. There was also a personal transition looming on the horizon. My marriage had been floundering for years and I was unhappy—we were *both* really unhappy. But I would never have thought to ask for a divorce.

I was taught that divorce was a sin. I was just sticking it out as best I could for the kids' sake, and grateful that I had a huge circle of friends in the community.

One day, out of the clear blue sky, Marty informed me he was moving out and filing for divorce. Although I was shocked, at the same time, I felt relieved. I know that divorce is never God's will or plan but sometimes it plays out that way in our human and imperfect lives. Neither of us was perfect and I know that I had my share of faults that led to his action.

It was a tragic day for me when they came for my car.

Uncertainty surfaced. I am now going down a new road; as a single mother with two young sons to provide for. Would my Tupperware part-time income be enough? Tightening my financial budget, I made it work as best I could. We didn't have any extra money, but once again I trusted God to provide.

Then the business transition happened. I had a dispute with the owners of the local Tupperware distributorship. From then on, it was a downhill slide that ended with them terminating my independent contractor agreement. It was a tragic day for me when they came for my car—an event that devastated me and left me in despair. I felt wronged and kicked aside—how could they do this to me? My excellent track record of sales didn't count for anything.

Another valuable lesson was learned:

Life is not always fair. Business failures happen.
People are sometimes treated with prejudice
and discrimination.

I hadn't yet realized that with God, transition is a necessary part of His plan for success. My Tupperware days were over, but they gave me the framework for my ultimate business success. I would later be grateful for the dismissal from a job I had loved doing.

3

Network Marketing Transitions Your Skills

Out of a job and unsure of what to do next, I again prayed for guidance. One day I got a call from one of the Vice Presidents of Tupperware who was also a good friend. He informed me that he had left Tupperware to accept a management position with a new network marketing company. He wondered if I might be interested in joining the company as a distributor.

I had never heard of network marketing or how it worked, so once again, I had to be willing to learn something new ... and I was and I did. I learned that in this new-to-me industry, some people were making very large amounts of monthly income. It was a financial system based on recruiting a few people who in turn recruited a few more—and those recruited would recruit even more. If this duplication went down through many levels, a substantial amount of monthly income could be earned by receiving a small amount of commission from each person's sales.

This system of marketing has created many millionaires over time within many different companies and I spent several years in this industry trying to achieve financial success. One of the companies had a product that was both dynamic and easy to sell. Called Derma Shield, it came in a can and squirted out a substance similar to shaving cream. By rubbing it all over your hands like a lotion and then letting it dry for a few minutes, a protective shield was formed that prevented chemicals from penetrating the shield. It found great success within hospitals and utility workers. Derma Shield protected hospital employees' allergic reactions to latex gloves as well as providing for bacteria protection. It was also a godsend to the workers who climbed the telephone poles; they routinely got burned with creosote on a daily basis.

I had great fun getting up in front of crowds doing a presentation because it was so dramatic. As I stood in front of a group, I would take a piece of tinfoil and put it over a glass and then coat my hands with Derma Shield. I had a small container with a dropper of hydrochloric acid, which was very dangerous and could burn through your skin on contact. The demonstration consisted of putting a few drops of the hydrochloric acid on top of the tin foil. Immediately, streaming black smoke was generated as it instantly burned a hole right through the foil. My audience was mesmerized by my demonstration. When I put the same acid drops in the palm of my hand, letting it sit for a full minute, it wasn't uncommon to hear gasps within the crowd. To their surprise, nothing happened—there would be no burn and no smoke because the protective shield prevented the acid from getting through. People would "ooh" and "ahhh" and marvel over this product. Needless to say, it was a revolutionary and wonderful product to promote.

I had developed recruiting skills which God had blessed me with during my Tupperware experience, and I carried those same abilities into this new industry. I was able to develop a very large organization of people and attain a regional manager level of achievement. Eventually, it was sold to a big commercial company.

Because I had initial success in this industry, I did several more programs over the next few years involving network marketing, including two telecommunications companies that were promoting lower long distance rates to customers.

As I reflect back today, I can so clearly see God's hand on my life. Each new transition brought me new learning experiences and gained me knowledge skills that would be invaluable to me down the road.

The first one was with a division of MCI. Once again, I built a large network of distributors who obtained new customers for MCI. We all got paid a little bit on those long distance bills. I felt this was a solid company and as long distance rates were too high, it was a win-win situation. I excelled well enough to be promoted to a regional manager and was in charge of overseeing the entire Western region for event marketing. I would travel to fairs, festivals, sporting events, etc., to help set up booths and obtain new customers.

MCI was very generous and gave away a lot of gifts to the public for switching service. During the time I was with them, its main competitor was AT&T. Prior to the landmark court decision allowing MCI into the market, AT&T had a monopoly on all long distance calls. It was a good move on the part of MCI to use a network marketing approach to gain market share, which it did successfully.

Eventually, MCI discontinued the division I was connected to, and once again, I was searching for what was next in God's plan for me. It came with one more networking opportunity of long distance. Excel Telecommunications came into my life, a company that was very similar to MCI, but had a much better income payout. I worked with them for a few years and did well. Excel made so many millions of dollars that the owner finally sold the company, ending all network marketing positions.

As I reflect back today, I can so clearly see God's hand on my life. Each new transition brought me new learning experiences and gained me knowledge skills that would be invaluable to me down the road. I had been on a steep learning curve—I was learning how to:

- Sell products and services;
- Build an organization of people and develop teamwork; and
- Understand the importance of leadership skills.

But most of all, I was learning to rely on God and trust in Him no matter what came my way. I learned that disappointments will come but need not define my life or when money is scarce—trust and have faith, He will provide. I needed to understand marketing and how to strategize to maximize potential. I felt His favor even through the struggles and discouraging times I had experienced.

All of these ventures allowed me to work part time and be available to my children while they were growing up. Our needs were always met, even though there were times when I didn't know where the next dollar was coming from. One door would close. Another would open.

Network marketing has a controversial side. It is still going strong today, more than 30 years later. There are hundreds of companies that promise great wealth and have hundreds, if not thousands, of products a person could sell. Because I worked in this arena for many years, I feel qualified to have, and to express, an opinion.

In general, there are few good companies with the ingredients necessary for success for the average person. The two main ingredients are an exceptional product or service and a truly unique compensation plan. It's the difference between success—and survival—and just being a flash in the pan. I saw many succeed financially beyond their dreams; and I saw others fail miserably. It is very difficult for the average person to have the mind set and skill to recruit enough people to make the duplication work as it is intended. It is also extremely difficult to make a living from it unless you are a high-powered and influential recruiter. The ones who did succeed were not part-timers for long—they created a full-time plan to follow and stuck to it.

Networking marketing can be a great way to add supplemental income to a family needing just a little more money to get by. I advise you to research carefully and pray earnestly for God's direction should you decide to give this area a try.

For me, God used it as a part of His marvelous and wonderful plan that led to my ultimate business success.

4

Tax Resolution—It Opened My Eyes

This part of my story is one of the most important in viewing God's hand on my journey to success. It emphasizes how God takes the most unlikely circumstances along with putting the most unlikely people in your path and orders your steps.

It started with something as simple as glancing through the help wanted ads of the newspaper one day out of curiosity. My eye fell on a small ad that read: Legal assistant wanted for law firm; no experience required. Without a shadow of a doubt, it was God who directed my eyes to pick up the paper that particular day and see that particular ad. I had no idea what law firm it was or what kind of law was practiced. I had no clue as to the position or what it entailed. But I had always had a keen interest in the field of law. I loved lawyer movies, books and trials. I served on jury duty a couple of times and loved it. I watched the OJ Simpson trial every single day on television and was fascinated. I had no desire, however, to spend the money or time (even if I had it) to go to law school.

I was currently working in the corporate office of a major grocery store chain. They had insurance kiosks in all their stores and were interested in developing a pre-paid legal plan for all their customers to enroll in should they ever have a legal problem. Through a close friend at church, I got an interview and was hired to head up that project. I was excited and a little scared at the same time. It was a position that was over my head but I believed in myself and my abilities to do new things.

I researched pre-paid legal plans, helped put a team of attorneys together for a panel and drafted a brochure and rates. It was a fun and rewarding. I had an office on the top floor with all the other executives and developed a natural friendship with the CEO of the company—he was a strong Christian as I was. Unfortunately, due to corporate cutbacks, the program was eliminated and, as a result, so was I. Hence that action necessitating my search that day into the want ads.

I had been told by my friends that I should have been an attorney because I have a quick, logical and argumentative mind and strong abilities of persuasion. I am also bold and courageous, which I inherited from my Dad. He taught me early on, that you always stand up for what you believe in and never back down. I could represent a client with ferocious tenacity if I had to. But, alas, being an attorney was not God's plan for me. It was close though.

Answering the ad, I got an appointment for the next day. It happened to be the Law Office of Roni Deutch. The position happened to be one of financial analysis of a prospective client, which translated simply meant "sales." The field of law involved was tax resolution. I had no idea what tax resolution was nor had I ever heard of Roni Deutch. I went for the interview and met with Roni's brother who was the supervisor in charge of sales. He liked my sales experience and took me to meet Roni in her office. Evidently she liked me as well, and I was hired on the spot.

Tax Payers Need Advocates

My eyes were opened—I learned a great deal about owing taxes to the Internal Revenue Service. Like the vast majority of Americans, I never knew that there was a program whereby the IRS would settle your tax liability for a fraction of what was owed. I had never owed anything on my taxes so was totally unfamiliar with tax liability in general. I was shocked to discover there are literally hundreds of thousands of people who end up owing money to the IRS each year. The reasons are many and varied, ranging from claiming too many deductions on their paystub (in order to have more income each month) to taking a distribution from a 401k plan with no tax being withheld. A common one for many is the situation of the self-employed. They often work as independent contractors. Rarely in that case is anyone's tax withheld, and at the end of the year, they are in trouble. They haven't disciplined themselves to save for what they owe in April.

I was also shocked to discover that tax liability covers all walks of life, and all income levels. There are doctors, lawyers, corporate executives, nurses, engineers, movie stars and people like you and me. It didn't matter what the income level was or the level of education. I learned there are many options available to help resolve this issue, and the proper course of action depended on their financial situation. Through a brief training period, I learned how to evaluate a taxpayer's financial data. It all centered around two areas: their assets with equity and their monthly income and expenses. Once I learned this system the IRS uses, it was easy to be able to analyze a taxpayer's situation and determine the right action to take for them.

When I started my job at the law firm, there were about 20 other sales people doing the same thing each day. We spent the entire day taking calls from people who needed help and doing a financial evaluation to see what kind of resolution they qualified for. If they happened to qualify for a settlement offer of some kind, that was the ultimate resolution because it literally wiped out most all of their debt. If they didn't qualify for that program, then it might be some kind of installment plan where they paid so much a month for five or six years until it was all paid.

As I did this day after day, I fell in love with this kind of work. Each person had a new and different story to tell and many were calling in tears and living in fear of the IRS. Many more had their wages garnished or their bank account cleaned out by the IRS. The general perception, and with good reason, is that the IRS is a feared and hated entity because of their harsh and brutal treatment of taxpayers. They tend to show a cold and uncaring attitude to taxpayers and their circumstances.

I remember reading about an especially horrible incident. The IRS went into a home with guns drawn terrorizing the family, only to find out it was the wrong house. Incidents like this and others caused Congressional hearings to occur. Many don't know that the IRS has no oversight and answers only to Congress. The result is that there is great latitude for behavior that would be totally unacceptable in other agencies. After many days of testimony, the IRS was publically scolded and new policies were set in place. They were to become a kinder, gentler, IRS.

Congress set in place a special department called the Taxpayer Advocates Office. Taxpayers who were having problems with IRS agents in getting resolution could call that office and get help at no charge. This was a giant step in progress towards fair treatment for taxpayers. These agents were not part of the IRS and were not accountable to anyone within the IRS, making it a separate agency. This new department was also accountable to Congress. In an effort to promote a climate of change for the better within the IRS, Congress mandated an annual report to be given to them each year on the most serious issues that needed to be addressed. This has been done now for many years and is truly a wonderful program, because they nail these problems within the IRS and highlight them for all to see. Many positive changes have come down through the years because of this annual report.

The more I worked with these painfully hurting taxpayers, the more dedicated I was to my job. I was contributing to making a huge difference in people's lives. It only took me a matter of weeks until I was one of the top sales people. I also loved the fact that we could dress casually for work; shorts in the summer and jeans in the winter—no more business suits and high heels. Even though I was now working a full time job, my sons were grown and out on their own. Each had gone his own way; my oldest to Dallas, Texas, where he received a degree in computer animation and now designed kid's video games. He was married and had a little girl. My youngest son had gone into the Marines.

Mistakes

Even though I was a solid Christian and loved the Lord with all my heart, on occasion (as we all do) I made mistakes that took me out of God's perfect will for my life. When that happened, I paid the price and the results caused a detour from God's plan for me. None of us are perfect and as Christians committed to following Christ, we oftentimes give in to what we want, not what God wants for us. I am no exception and it's important to be transparent about our own mistakes.

God's word tells us that Satan constantly tempts us to sin and makes it attractive and hard to say "No" to. This happens on a regular basis as Satan works hard to undermine Christians and the work of the Lord. He is successful far too much of the time. But thankfully, God is a forgiving God and greater is He that is in us, than he that is in the world. Ever since I was a child, my favorite scripture has been Romans 8:28 which tells us that **all things** will work together for good to them who love Him.

My father had taught me as a teenager that God's word commands a Christian not to be unequally yoked together with an unbeliever in marriage. For that reason I was not allowed to even date a non-Christian when I was in high school. I met my first husband, Marty, my senior year of high school and he was not a Christian. When he asked me out on a date, I told him I could not go out with him. I was a little embarrassed to have to explain why, but my Dad did allow me to invite him to church. The very first time he came to church, after hearing my father preach that Sunday evening, he walked forward and accepted Christ as his personal savior. It was a precious moment and even though we ended up divorcing years later, I will always be proud that I was able to show him the way to Christ.

Spiritual Disharmony

Now, many years later, I was working at the Law Office of Roni Deutch, was single and my children were grown. I wanted to date so I joined a dating service called Great Expectations. I wrote out my profile declaring my faith and personality traits and asked God to lead me to the right person. I dated several men over the course of a few months who were all very attractive and nice men. None of them seemed to get my attention.

One day I got a notice in the mail that someone had picked me out of the books and wanted to meet me. I went in to look at his picture and read his profile—he was good looking, had a very interesting profile and liked some of the same things I did. It revealed that he was a therapist and counselor. I couldn't see that he was a Christian from reading about him, but decided to give him a date and see where it would go. Meeting for dinner one evening, we discovered that we had a lot to talk about, but, it became clear to me that he was not a Christian and did not have any idea of what it meant to have a personal relationship with Jesus Christ.

My father's words of caution were lost in the moment— I liked him and so I continued to date him. Being upfront about my faith and how important it is to me is who I am and I didn't hold back. He said he understood but didn't share my views. I felt that if he went to church and heard the word,

God would touch his heart and he would accept Christ. To my delight, he agreed to go to church with me. And each time we attended, he would say he really enjoyed it and liked my pastor. I used those occasions to try and gently steer him in the direction of Christ.

I ended up dating him for over four years, but didn't succeed in leading him to Christ—I also ended up falling in love with him. This is precisely why my Dad said to never date a non-Christian. You run the risk of falling in love and then find yourself in an impossible situation spiritually. I followed the biblical method of living a Christ centered life and being the best role model I could. I was never pushy or aggressive in our discussions, but gentle and loving. His heart was hardened and although at times he asked questions about the Bible, he would never accept God's answers.

I want to acknowledge to you that I have, at times, strayed from His will, but that our God is a God of forgiveness, mercy and grace.

Being in the Center of God's Will

When you truly desire to be in the center of God's will and plan for your life, and your spiritual relationship with Him is good, then when you begin to stray outside His will, He warns you. I was heading down the wrong road with this relationship and God used several ways to warn me over these four years. This man I was dating began to exhibit behaviors that were unacceptable in a committed relationship, not once but many times. I heard God speaking to me that this was not the man for me loud and clear. I was getting outside the blessings and favor that God places on His children who are obedient to His word.

Nevertheless, my human need of being loved kept getting in the way. My fleshly desires made me weak in my obedience to my Lord. I ignored the warnings even though they continued to come in different ways and at different times. With each one, I knew what God was telling me. Yet, I chose to overlook them. When he finally asked me to marry him, I said yes. I rationalized this by continuing to believe I could eventually lead him to the Lord through prayer. Of course, this was totally wrong thinking on my part and there was no justification for disobedience to God's word.

I cite this personal example to you for several reasons. I want to acknowledge to you that I have, at times, strayed from His will, but that our God is a God of forgiveness, mercy and grace. I want to encourage you to continue to trust in Him when you stray, as Satan has a hand in these times and loves nothing more than to get you way out of God's will and favor. Satan knows our weakest areas and uses them to great advantage. I believe we need to have a greater awareness of his strategies and antics in our fight against him. We need to "put on the whole armor of God" daily. But most importantly, I want you to know that even your mistakes can be used for your good and there can be a happy ending. Because we "know that **all things** work together for good ..." somewhere down the road of life.

I married Dick and we had some good years ... we went to church together once a month or so, but mostly I went alone. I continued to witness to him about the Lord but his heart remained as hard as rock. When you are unequally yoked together, you don't have a spiritual compatibility. This now spills over into many other areas of life because things that a Christian knows is wrong, a non-Christian doesn't. He did things that were definitely not God honoring but I never preached at him. I did express my views and prayed for him daily. It was hard when we were out with his friends, who shared his values, because I was the lone Christian. I was vocal about my faith, but there were many very uncomfortable situations I encountered. Many times I wondered why God had allowed me to be in this situation, to fall in love with someone who was obviously not of my faith.

The Power of Prayer

Because I have lived for many years experiencing the power of prayer and how awesome and marvelous answered prayers are. I decided to ask God for help in demonstrating His power to my husband—the man that I had fallen in love with and married.

There were two distinct times that I attempted to show him the power of prayer and thus impact his heart for an awareness of God. The first was when we went salmon fishing early one morning down at the river. There were literally hundreds of men casting lines and jockeying for a good position on the bank while it was still dark outside. He loved to fish and I went along to watch. After standing there for a couple of hours and catching nothing, he was getting discouraged. The salmon were running and other fishermen were catching them.

So, I prayed right then and there that God would let him catch a salmon and that it would be a big one. I prayed for God to allow this answer to prayer in order to demonstrate His power and presence. Not five minutes after I began my prayer, he caught a huge salmon. He was so excited, but he did not know of my personal prayer on his behalf. Once he got the fish out of the water, I was so excited to tell him what God had done in His answer. I explained to him he caught the fish solely because I prayed for it and God answered. To my utter amazement, he completely discounted this explanation. I was so angry that he could be so dense and hardened and not see what was right in front of his eyes. He bragged about the fish for months, but never gave any credit to my prayer.

Another time, we took a weekend trip to the Russian River in Northern California for a concert. It was held on the bank of the river and there were hundreds of people. We had a good spot right at the water's edge. He had taken off his shorts and put his wallet in a pocket, before he got in the water to cool off. At the end of the day when he put them back on, he noticed his wallet was gone. We just knew someone had stolen it as there were so many people in a small area of beach.

We looked everywhere, but it was nowhere to be found— everything was gone—credit cards, driver's license and what cash we had—we were both upset. Returning to our hotel, we had to borrow money for dinner from the friends we were with. As we started to get ready for bed, the Lord seemed to tell me to pray again but this time, tell Dick about what I was going to do. And I did. I told him I was going to show him the power of prayer one more time and I prayed for his wallet to turn up. This would have to be a miracle because no one knew where we were staying, and we were from out of town.

Around midnight, the phone rang. It was the front desk saying a man was there asking to speak with Dick. Frankly, I was a little scared—why would anyone be asking for us late at night like that? He got dressed and went down to the office. Within fifteen minutes, he was back with a smile spread across his face and his wallet in his hand. All his credit cards were there, the cash and his driver's license. Even though I had prayed for this, it was still so amazing, I could hardly believe it.

The man told how he and a friend were boating down the river and saw something floating in the water. It was floating much further down than where we had been sitting. They fished it out of the water, looked at the ID and saw that we lived in Sacramento, over three hours away. They deduced we had to be in town for the music festival, so they drove up and down the main street asking at every hotel if there was someone registered there by our name.

Wow! Talk about answered prayer. That was a miracle. It was a miracle that it floated and didn't sink to the bottom; it was a miracle that honest men found it; and it was a miracle that they cared enough to search every hotel in town for us to return it. I was so totally in awe of God's power and might. He is so good.

"Dick, what do you think about God answering my prayers?" I asked him.

"It wasn't God," was his response. "Anyone could have found it and there was nothing unusual about a man turning it in."

I was stunned, even dumbfounded, with his reaction. The anger that welled up in me led to a very big argument—I could hardly get to sleep. I had never experienced this hard of a heart in a person. This was the second time I had specifically prayed for God to show him proof of His word and presence. It would be the last time I would do it—it was clear that my husband was not a man of faith.

The lesson from this very major mistake I made by getting outside of God's will was a hard one.

I prayed for his salvation and continue to this day to pray for it. Unless he connects with God and opens his blind eyes, he will die without the opportunity to live in eternity with Christ. This is tragic to me and horrifying. I hope God sees fit to answer that prayer of mine before it's too late.

The lesson from this very major mistake I made—by getting outside of God's will—was a hard one. It brought personal grief and anguish, not the love I so desired. Don't get me wrong, we had a lot of good times and experiences together. I had my own share of faults so I don't lay all the blame on him. It wasn't all bad, but the lack of spiritual compatibility took a huge toll on me. There was no one to pray with, no one to rejoice with when God answered prayer, no one to read and discuss the Bible with and no one to sit in church with me as a couple should. Being alone at church became a very sore spot for me. It got to where I had to plead and beg for him to accompany me.

Still, when you make a mistake, you ask for forgiveness, and move on with God's grace and mercy. I had already made one mistake and wasn't about to compound it with another divorce. So I hung in there, and prayed for strength.

My job at the law firm was really going well and I was making a lot of money. For over three years, I was extremely happy there and loved what I did. Seeing some settlement offers come in for the clients I helped bring on board was wonderful and so satisfying. God's hand was still on my life and my mistakes did not reverse His wonderful and marvelous plan for me.

5

The Birth of Tax Tiger

After four years working at the Law Office of Roni Deutch, the working environment was becoming oppressive—at times, downright demeaning. There were things happening that caused our sales group great concern. For me, some of these concerns were egregious. Roni had hired the son of the man her mother was dating to be in charge of the collections department, claiming that Scott was her "brother." Scott would call clients who were behind in sending in their monthly payment, beginning a string of harassing calls which caused a huge uproar with the firm's clients. None of us could miss overhearing the verbal abuse; his desk was positioned close enough to us so that we could clearly hear his every word.

Many of these conversations were rude and threatening. Ironically, it felt to me like the IRS was calling them—listening to these conversations all day long—the very thing that we were supposed to be relieving them of when they became our clients. It became a very real issue for many of us. We couldn't do a good job talking to clients about our services with Scott using very threatening, demeaning and obnoxious language that we and our clients could hear at the same time.

One day I got a call from an irate husband. This family was one that I had just brought on as a client a few months before. They really liked me and he was calling to tell me that Scott had called and threatened his wife for a payment that was one day late. He had reduced her to tears and she was very frightened. I remember the husband saying, "This kind of action better never happen again." Of course; it shouldn't have happened in the first place. Apologizing profusely, I hung up the phone and went to see my manager.

> *Asking for a personal meeting with Roni was a very risky thing to do because many of her employees were afraid of her and her explosive temper.*

Nepotism was woven throughout the organization. My manager was one of Roni's three brothers (this time, a real one) who agreed with me that this was unacceptable behavior. I had previously tried to talk to Scott on my own before this incident, to make him see how his actions were affecting not only us but the clients. It was a horrible image to portray to the public. True to form, he was rude and arrogant and gave no consideration to anything I said. I asked for a personal meeting with Roni to discuss this. Asking for any type of meeting with Roni was a very risky thing to do because many of her employees were afraid of her and her explosive temper. She shouted and used offensive language at sales meetings and would threaten to fire all of us if our sales goals were not met.

I was one of the "lucky" ones, meaning that I brought in plenty of revenue for the company. If your sales were as high as mine always were, she was friendly. Money talked to Roni. As long as my sales were high, I had always had a good relationship with her. Also, I was the only one who consistently brought in full payment accounts and Western Union payments which she advocated. Winning many awards and recognition during my years of employment, I didn't have the "Roni Fear" that so many of my colleagues had. I felt she needed to know what was happening to our clients and Scott's horrendous behavior with them, as well as subjecting the rest of the office to his mean and arrogant client phone calls.

Finally, I was able to explain the situation to her. To my relief, she seemed appalled at such behavior, stating, "It was never my intention to treat clients this way and I will have a talk with him."

I felt good about this and thought the matter would be resolved and told the others so ... It was not resolved.

Oh, she did, as promised, talk to him. The outcome was that it made him very angry at me. He tempered some of his language for short time and then it was back to business as usual. Our only recourse at this point was to ask the manager to move him to a place where we couldn't hear him talking on the phone to our clients. His negativity was affecting our ability to bring in new clients.

*It was always about production
and maximum performance,
no matter what.*

Complaints started to come in from existing clients who paid for their service and never got it resolved. I didn't know the details of any of the cases so I had no idea of the truthfulness of these claims. I just continued to do my job, the one that I was hired for, which meant selling the services of Roni Deutch.

Her company continued to grow during the years I was there. We moved to a brand new building and the work force was expanded—many new employees were hired. But with those changes also came changes that to me were detrimental to the mental and emotional health of the employees. Roni became very dictatorial. At one staff meeting, she told us we were not allowed to speak to each other in the kitchen or in the restrooms. This was bizarre and I raised my hand and questioned it during this meeting. She restated her command: no speaking to each other in the kitchen or restroom. We had to sign out for our breaks and if we were one minute late in returning, we were reprimanded and the same went for lunch breaks. There was no leeway. The joy I had felt when I first started at Roni Deutch's company was quickly evaporating.

The straw that broke the camel's back was a new software tool that some salesperson probably convinced her would increase production. For her, it was always about production and maximum performance, no matter what. This new software program would track your telephone calls each day. It recorded how many minutes you were on each call, how many minutes between calls, and a total number of hours of talk time at the end of the day.

Daily tracking commenced—the number of hours of talk time would be listed on a sheet and placed on the wall for all to see. If you didn't talk long enough, you would be called in and reprimanded. I'm sure there are many large companies who use this method, but it can be abusive, oppressive and grossly unfair to good people who get caught up in it. There was no notation for the number of new cases that signed up— it was only and all about "talk time."

For me, it was a nightmare. The average time it took me to do a free consultation and financial analysis was approximately 30 minutes, which was enough time for me to do it accurately and completely. Because God had blessed me with good people skills, I didn't need to take as long as the other sales people. There were now around 45 of us—hundreds of leads—prospects—were calling daily from the television commercials Roni aired. Where I took 30 minutes, the majority of the sales staff took an hour or so to complete each of their consultations. I could easily do two consultations and sign the client on, in the same amount of time, where others would often have to do follow-up phone calls requiring even more time.

Suddenly, I found my name at the bottom of the list every day because I had the least amount of talk time. But I also had the highest number of sales, the highest number of clients who paid in full and high numbers of those who used Western Union to send payment. These were the areas Roni focused on in our department. I excelled in all of them. I brought the greatest amount of revenue into her firm consistently. Now, I am getting called into the supervisor's office each day to be counseled on my talk time being too low. I explained the situation and how I got all my calls done each day.

It didn't matter! I was still considered deficient, and finally, they started a policy of writing up a person whose talk time was too low. This made no logical or business sense. I could easily have just talked longer to each person, but that was awkward for me, unnecessary and a waste of time. One day around lunch time, I was called into the office and issued a citation; I was told if I didn't take corrective action, I would be terminated. This was so unbelievable that I was shocked. For a company to fire their top sales person for something so ridiculous was ludicrous and showed how little top performance was valued. It was totally irrational from both a business and a personal sense. I sat in my car that day at lunch and cried.

He said, "Kathy, you don't need to work for someone like that. You've been there for over four years and know what you're doing. Just start your own business!"

Looking back, I now know what was happening. Joel Osteen reaches over seven million viewers weekly. His books have been read in over 100 countries. Count me as one of his biggest fans. I recalled one of the stories he shared in a sermon. His story depicts an event that is common in the springtime:

Before a mother bird has babies, she builds a nest. She builds it with twigs and bits of cloth or paper towels or soft material to cover the sharpness of the twigs.

When the babies are born, they rest snuggled in the nest with the mother caring for them, bringing them food and protecting them as they grow. When they are ready to leave the nest, she must teach them to fly, so she starts gradually taking out the soft pieces of the nest.

Gradually, the nest becomes uncomfortable to the fledglings. Finally, when the sharp twigs begin to poke and hurt the babies enough, they jump from the nest and discover that their little wings can help them fly. The secret of their success: They were pushed from the nest only when the mother bird knew they were ready and could fly on their own.

Remembering the story, I could feel God speak to my heart, telling me it was He pushing me from the comfort of my nest. Through tears that afternoon, I realized that He was telling me that it was time to fly. Wow, what a lesson for us all.

I went home that evening very upset and discouraged. I didn't understand how God could allow something like this to happen, when I loved what I was doing and was making good money for both myself and for my employer. But God's hand was on my life. After hearing what had transpired, my husband, Dick, said something to me that was both surprising and prophetic. It was my burning bush moment. He said, "Kathy, you don't need to work for someone like that. You've been there for over four years and know what you're doing. Just start your own business!" I looked at him in amazement.

"Me, start my own business?" I replied. I could never do that because to negotiate with the IRS you needed to be a CPA, an attorney, or an enrolled agent. I was none of those three.

That didn't faze him at all. He said, "You don't need to be one of those three. Just hire them to work for you."

Instantly the light bulb went on in my head. Yes, I could hire professionals to work for me. Even though there were problems in our marriage, Dick was always supportive of my efforts and abilities. I will be forever grateful to him for saying those words to me that day, because I would never have thought of them myself. In that instant, Tax Tiger was born. God's hand was on my life in a very big way.

God spoke to my heart, telling me it was He pushing me from the comfort of my nest. Through tears that afternoon, I realized that He was telling me that it was time to fly. As God told Moses He would be with him and teach him what to say and do, I felt He was saying the same to me. God gave me another scripture found in Isaiah 41:10 which reads, "So do not fear, for I am with you; do not be dismayed, for I am your God. I will strengthen you and help you; **I will uphold you with my righteous right hand.**

Power of Prayer

I felt strongly that God was calling me to a plan of action that was scary and way beyond my ability—the ability to run my own business. I went to God in prayer over and over on a multitude of areas. I told Him that if this truly was His will for my life, He would need to work out all the pieces for me. There was so much to do, and so many parts to the puzzle of creating a business; I didn't know where to start. Here was yet another transition.

With some research on my competition on the Internet, I learned that there were primarily three mega firms in my field. These three companies were national companies making many millions of dollars a year. All of them had many complaints filed against them: Roni Deutch, J.K. Harris and Tax Masters. I was intrigued; after further exhaustive search, I could not find one company of any major size who had a reputation of quality work and customer service and with only few complaints.

My first objective was to put together a business plan to take to the bank to get a startup loan. After looking on the Internet for some help in this area, I hired a company which touted great results helping people to write successful business plans. Paying them $2,000 to become their client, I began to list the key components of the plan as I was instructed to do. I had watched Roni Deutch bring in thousands of leads a month with a TV commercial that I didn't think was all that good. How hard could it be to create a better one?

My husband was against hiring any company online—he believed we would get "ripped off." Instead, we should look for someone local that we could meet face-to-face and get references from within the community. Instead, however, I pressed for using the company I had engaged online, and so we did. But, the weeks turned into months and no business plan was produced. Sadly to say, Dick was right.

We did not always agree on business decisions but on this issue, he was on the mark. I lost my money because they went out of business—they notified me by e-mail. Now I had no business plan, $2,000 less in my bank account and was back to square one.

God told me to just trust Him and believe.

I sat in tears at my kitchen table that day, devastated by this first setback, a huge one. Remember, Satan attacks mightily when a Christian is being obedient. I'm sure this was designed to make me give up. I put in a call to David, my son, in Texas; he had been a rock of support for me on this new road I was traveling down. I was computer illiterate, and he had been patiently helping me to learn some basics. I had consulted with him many times as I worked to learn to use the computer and he always answered my questions as completely as he could. I am so blessed to have him as a son. He responded very calmly to my tears by telling me that I could buy a software program which would help me create a business plan myself. He even looked up the best one for me and told me where and what to order.

I continued to pray for guidance and direction as I worked through this—for me—difficult job of designing a business plan, something that I had never done before. I had faith in God's plan and His word that tells us if we have faith as a "grain of mustard seed" it will be done. I felt in my heart this was right, but I still had no clue as to how I was going to carry it out. I felt like Moses when God chose him to lead the Israelites out of slavery and to the Promised Land. Moses told the Lord that there was "no way." He was not capable, and he stuttered his refusal. God as the wise mentor told Moses, "I will go with you; I will give you the words to say."

God uses the weak to confound the strong. I did not have a college degree and I had no formal business education. What I did have, however, was considerable "in the trenches" business experience in the area I was planning to enter and start a business.

God told me to trust Him and believe. He would direct my steps. His hand was on this business plan. So I kept on and finally the business plan was as polished and complete as I could get it. I had it reviewed by a professional business consultant who thought it was very good. Armed with that plan, I set out with it and my immense enthusiasm, to meet with a bank manager. I was seeking a $50,000 start-up loan,

Much to my amazement—and disappointment—I was turned down. My plan was solid, but I needed more collateral. I went to the Small Business Administration which had the reputation of giving a priority to women seeking business loans. No, they don't; not without sufficient collateral. I went from bank to bank and was turned down every time. I found that it was going to be impossible to get a loan without collateral, no matter how good my plan was. I was applying in my name only. I did not want to include my husband in any obligation for the repayment of the business loan I was seeking. When we married, the house was his, and I did not want to risk his equity, if my business venture failed. I know this was not a matter of faith, but it was practical and fair.

When the last bank said, "No," I was out of options. But again I was reminded by God in Psalm 89:21, "**My hand** will sustain him; surely my arm will strengthen him. I knew God's strength was about to come from somewhere unexpected. Then my husband sat me down and told me we needed to put up his house as collateral. He encouraged me to agree with this; it was necessary, or we would not be able to move forward. He said he believed in me and we would be successful. The loan was for only a relatively small amount so I reluctantly agreed. He also wanted to be my business partner 50/50, although he would not be working in the business. He had a full time job as principle of a special education school and made a good income. I agreed, and we went back to the bank and applied again, this time with the house as the necessary collateral.

A God Story

There are many stories from this point on that I call God stories. They are amazing circumstances and answers to prayer that only God could control. They demonstrate clearly how God's hand was on my business.

I was astonished that there was a space available. This was a prime property and those tenants never gave up any space and moved out.

54

While I was waiting to see if this loan application would be approved, I started looking for office space. I looked all over Sacramento and couldn't find anything that felt right to me. I needed to start small with something we could afford. I wanted to be by water somehow, as I love all water: lakes, streams, rivers, and oceans. There is a major river running through downtown Sacramento and a couple of small lakes, but no office space that was affordable in any of those areas.

I normally looked in the newspapers classified section during the week for office space that was available. One Sunday morning, right before church, I was looking at the paper, and God spoke to me; He told me to look in the office space section. This was unusual and I would normally have waited until Monday to resume my search. (But God must have known that Sunday is an excellent want-ad day.) Feeling "led," I did as I was asked, and my eye fell on a new ad that I had never seen before. It was for office space on Lake Greenhaven.

Greenhaven?! I almost fell out of my chair. I knew of Lake Greenhaven because I lived in a condo on that very lake before Dick and I were married. It was not so much a lake as it was a waterway that wove through a very upscale neighborhood. It was designed to extend past the backyard of each home as the yard faced the water but it was still invisible from the street. It was as though the community had a private channel that few knew about unless they lived there. In addition, the Sacramento River was just across the street and a couple of blocks away.

I had loved living in my condo backed up to this waterway, and I even had a small paddle boat. There were palm trees and it looked like Florida when you gazed out the window. It was a beautiful visual, and because I had lived there for a few years after selling my home, I knew of the office building with the advertised rental. It was the only office building on this lake, tucked into this residential neighborhood. What a find!

I was astonished that there was a space available. This was a prime property and those tenants never gave up any space and moved out. They had all been there for years. But **where God guides, God provides**. I called the phone number in the ad and asked to be the very first one to look at the space on Monday morning. The property manager said there had been many calls, but she would schedule me first. I walked into that office Monday morning and stopped dead in my tracks. It was the most beautiful space I had ever seen. There was a huge room with floor-to-ceiling windows looking out on the water. There were three other smaller rooms also facing the water, two of them with decks. There was one other room which did not face the water, and there was a reception area. There would be enough space for a conference/staff room, a reception area, and four offices.

It was perfect. This was our space. I felt an immediate peace that God would somehow give this space to us.

Then the property manager quoted me a rental amount. It was truly a prime location—and, as such, the rent was higher than I had factored into my budget. But it didn't matter; I knew I wanted this office space. My dilemma was the fact that my bank loan had not yet been approved. Without that, I would have no business. I stepped out in faith once again, believing that it would be approved and God's hand was on it. I explained to the property manager that my loan was about to be approved but I couldn't sign a lease until it was, and asked her if she would hold the space for me for a couple of weeks.

This was absolutely not done in property management. They did not hold space, and besides, there were ten other people waiting behind me to see the space. She looked at me for a long moment, frowned a little, and said, "In all my 30 years in property management, I have never done this, but somehow I believe you just may be the right tenant for this space. If you will put down $1,000 as a deposit, I will hold the space for you for 30 days. If your loan doesn't come through, you will lose your deposit."

Had I not looked in the Sunday paper on that particular day, that awesome space would have been gone. That was no coincidence, but God's favor. I jumped for joy. Thank you, Jesus! I immediately took my checkbook out, gave her a check for $1,000 and raced home to tell my husband I had found the perfect office space. I wanted him to come back with me immediately and look at it. When I told him I had found the perfect space and written a check for $1,000 non-refundable deposit, he was very upset and said, "You did what? You should never put money down before you know if you have the loan."

There was that incompatibility of Christian faith surfacing again. However, when he saw the space, he was also impressed, and since it was my thousand dollars to lose, he didn't have much more to say.

Within two weeks, our loan was approved. I got the office space my heart had longed to have, and to this day, over ten years later, it still brings me joy every time I walk in the door. Every time a new client comes in for an appointment, they walk into the conference room and do a double take. It is so unusual and beautiful a room that time and time again clients comment on the beauty, warmth, and peacefulness they feel when they walk in. Their fear level and stress level start to lessen. This remains to this day one of my favorite God stories.

What's In a Name?

Now that we had the loan and the office space, we needed a name for the company. I prayed hard for God to lead us because I knew that whatever name we chose would be crucial to the success of our business. In marketing, the name of your business is vitally important if you want to stand out from all your competition and be sure clients remember you. I knew that I was not wise enough to come up with a good name. My husband wanted Hill and Hill—not outstanding. I nixed that idea, because who could remember that name? I went back to the internet to research name development companies and found one that stood out to me. They were called Name Sharks and had the picture of a shark as a logo.

They described how they use retired newspaper editors for their panel and will brainstorm names until they have one hundred name ideas to offer. I described the business of tax resolution, and they went to work. After a week I got the list of names and some tag lines for some of them—many were quite good. They also had a guarantee that if you didn't like any of them, they would do another hundred. As I read, one name jumped out at me: Tax Tiger. There was also a tag line which read, "We've earned our stripes." I loved this name and its tag line and knew a good tiger picture for a logo would be quite memorable to potential clients.

With a little persuasion, Dick agreed with me. Finally, we had our name. That choice would turn out to be one of the best business decisions we made. For the logo, I turned again to my son, David, the designer. He did several versions of a tiger for me until he came up with just the right one. We trademarked the tiger image and our name. This was God's hand on our business in a huge way. Tax Tiger, Inc., began in October 2002 on a glorious fall day. Can you see how God was preparing and teaching me a lot of what I needed throughout the early years of my life?

- I developed a strong faith and trust in Him;
- I went through several unpleasant transitions;
- I experienced the awesome power of prayer on a regular basis;
- I was willing to learn new things as they came to me;
- I gained important sales skills;
- I developed leadership ability;
- I was dedicated to being in the center of His will;
- I was able to acknowledge and ask forgiveness for mistakes;
- I gave Him praise and honor and glory for each blessing and bit of favor He bestowed on me;

- I sought guidance and wisdom when I didn't know what to do or where to turn; and
- I tried to be a vocal and sincere role model for my faith.

These are areas every Christian and business owner should strive to maintain. When you do, God's hand will be on your business.

6

In the Beginning

With the major components now in place, I needed to address personnel. The main employee I would need was an office manager/bookkeeper. I needed someone who was skilled in accounting and could keep the books and pay the bills as well as having top notch computer skills. I could do the sales, but I needed an office manager as well as a CPA or enrolled agent to work on the cases. God brought a fine Christian CPA to me, Randy, with whom I formed an alliance; he would process my case work on a commission basis. He had his own practice but agreed to take on my case work.

It was my primary desire to deliver top quality service with an excellence not found in the industry.

One of the other top sales agents who I worked with at Roni Deutch's office somehow got wind of what I was doing; she called and asked to come work for me. Things apparently were getting worse over there and she just couldn't take it any longer. Because she was very good, I agreed to hire her. Now I had two great sales people to bring in the clients.

I put an ad in the newspaper for an office manager and got over a hundred resumes. I was shocked at the number of applicants; that was back in the days before the job market took such a dive. I sorted through them and called in the top twenty for a personal interview. I couldn't pay a great salary as a brand new company, so it would have to be exactly the right person. I prayed over it and trusted God to give me the one. The very last resume I received was late coming in and I almost didn't include her. The main reason I did was that her resume showed some TV production experience. I felt that would come in handy when I began to develop my own TV commercial. Her name was Carla.

After nineteen interviews in two days, Carla was the last one to meet with me. I had a couple of good prospects but no one who really jumped out at me or gave me any peace of mind. When Carla walked into the room, that changed. I liked her immediately. As we started to talk and she shared with me all her experience and abilities, I knew she was the one. She wanted a little more than I could afford, but again, **where God guides, God provides**. I needed to be sure she could handle the huge task of getting a startup company off the ground. She was positive she could do the job, so I hired her. It was one of the best personnel decisions I ever made. Carla was fabulous.

She set to work helping me design and create forms, setting up QuickBooks for accounting, designing a website and many other necessary items. She gave me guidance on creating a TV commercial, which was crucial to our marketing ... or so I thought. Because Roni Deutch brought in thousands of leads a month with an average, so-so commercial, I knew I could do one better and wasn't even looking for the thousands of leads, just 50 to 75 a month to start. We focused on putting a great commercial together on a limited budget. We found a company that was local and could do it within our price range. We spent days writing scripts, and then filming it. When it was complete, we were all satisfied with the results.

Carla was a very important part of my early success and although she was not a Christian, she was a huge blessing to me.

It was my primary desire to deliver top quality service with an excellence not found in the industry. I wanted to continue to "make a difference in people's lives." It was, and still is, my main motto,

Making a difference in people's lives.

I did not have what I call the "greed factor" in my heart. This industry is rife with companies where greed is their driving force. My heart was in the right place, so I was trusting in Him for success and profit. My faith in myself and in God's plan for me was very strong. As I look back, I can see how critical that was.

Office Environment

The final important thing I needed to accomplish was to create an office environment such that one would love to come to work every day. I had never been in a work environment where I loved to go to work. I don't think there are many out there. I was determined to create an exceptional one. I started with the decorating. Remember, I am very fashion-oriented and color conscious. My home was that way and so would be my office. It was important to surround myself with beautiful things and colors that I love. Adding to my own productivity and creativity, the sense of feeling, experience and confidence balance naturally extended to both my staff and our clients.

The property manager agreed to paint all the walls, so I picked out paint. I requested wall paper and she paid for that as well. I mostly hung it myself, working late at night until I was exhausted. I picked out furniture for each office. There would be NO cubicles for my company—I hated working in a small cubicle. Each of my employees would have their own office, nicely decorated and inviting. After all, when we meet with clients, we wanted them to feel safe and comfortable. Each was experiencing financial stress and pressure. Would they lose their homes? Their jobs? Would their lives be destroyed by aggressive IRS tactics? Creating and maintaining an environment in which they felt welcome and that their needs would be met was at the top of my list.

And there was more. Along one side of the office was a built-in counter and cupboards which I used for a coffee and tea area. It worked beautifully and I've received many compliments on it. Our clients naturally move toward it to get that welcoming cup as they settle in for their appointments.

For my staff, I wanted them to feel that being part of the Tax Tiger team was not just another job—it was their work, and a place that was a joy to come to each day. Oh, there would be challenges. The nature of our work is enveloped by those challenges. But by creating a visual atmosphere that is calming for them and our clients, I knew that everyone could, and would, breathe just a little bit easier.

I chose not to implement the traditional sign-out sheet for breaks, lunch, the in and out each day. Instead, I gave them freedom to be there when they were supposed to be, and if they were a few minutes late, I never commented. With that freedom, came responsibility on their part. They knew they were accountable for not misusing and abusing my generosity. I believed people want to be treated like adults, not children, and will give you their best if they are well treated. I also paid for their lunch hour. They worked an eight-hour day with a half hour lunch. I paid them for the entire eight hours. Lunch was on me. I had never experienced that in any of the companies that I had worked for in the past. It has paid off very well for me in employee loyalty.

A birthday plan was created where on each employee's birthday, he or she was recognized the entire day with special things. I came in early to decorate his or her office with balloons and decorations. Lunch was catered; it included a "favorite" item that the birthday person loved, for the entire staff, one that included a lunch time birthday party with cards and gifts. The birthday celebrant has to sit in one of the recliners and wear a silly hat for pictures. All of us have so much fun—each person feels that this truly is a special day.

Post-it notes are handed out in various shapes ahead of time and everyone writes compliments about the birthday person (with no author names) and they are all read out loud and handed to them.

I also do a very nice Christmas party at the end of the year. It varies from year to year, but we reserve a nice restaurant for dinner, everyone dresses up and spouses are included. Everyone brings a nice gift for a gift exchange where we have a lot of fun and laughter by being able to snag someone else's gift for a few rounds. After dinner and the gift exchange, we have casino night where a professional company brings in real blackjack tables and we have contests. This is a very expensive night for me but I do it regardless of affordability.

Lastly, but probably most important, is how I treat them. I seldom wear the "boss hat" but treat them as co-workers and friends. We use the team approach as each of us, including me, is a member of the team and each position is as important as the next. This generates loyalty and exceptional performance. I have developed a work environment that I myself would love to come to and thus, they do as well.

Values

As I started this tiny, baby business, I determined to have the proper values front and center for both staff and clients to see. Values of honesty, integrity, quality customer service and having a focus on *making a difference in people's lives* were my priority. I was also committed to lifting up the Lord in the workplace and being the best testimony and role model I could be. I continued to pray for guidance and direction and yes, profit and success.

If there is one person who models values and makes no qualms about it, and consistently lives these godly values, it is one of my heroes, Tim Tebow, the former quarterback for the Denver Broncos and now the back-up quarterback for the NY Jets at this writing. I have loved him and his testimony for the Lord since I first saw him in a college game with the scripture John 3:16 in the black under his eyes. I thought, "Wow, what an amazing young man. I have followed him ever since and prayed for him and his courage to stand for his Lord despite any and all criticisms. When you stand for God, He will stand for you. This is what happened in 2011 as he played for the Denver Broncos. God stood with him, and millions of people saw him take a knee on the field when he made a great play. His attitude and giving personality towards those less fortunate are to be emulated and praised. His success is a direct result of desiring to stay in the center of God's will and holding tight to the values of God's word. No matter what is in store for Tim with football, God has a great and mighty plan for his life. This same thing is happening today with our Sirius radio commercial, heard by hundreds of thousands, which ends with the words, "We give to charity and all the glory to God." This commercial is a resounding success because we verbally lift up the Lord in our advertising. Few companies do this.

Soon after opening, I felt compelled to start a morning routine that I have continued to this day and one in which I am convinced put God's hand on my business success in a mighty way. Our office officially opens each day at 9:00. I make it a point to be there at 7:00—something that isn't difficult as I am a morning person anyway. My early morning routine consists of several things, including reading the newspaper with a cup of coffee.

Worship Music

Listening to worship music, both at church and at home is an extremely uplifting exercise spiritually. God created music and music is mentioned in many places in the Bible. For instance, Psalm 95:2 reads, "Let us come before him with thanksgiving and extol him with music and song." It will touch your heart and minister to your spirit. I'm not talking loud, hard rock style music either. I can't feel a worshiping attitude with that style. Worship music puts me in an immediate place of relationship and closeness with my heavenly Father. And I am reminded here that in the Old Testament, David's songs and harp provided peace and comfort for King Saul.

This is the first thing I do upon arriving at my office: In my conference room is a CD player and I have it loaded with six different worship tapes. I turn on the music and it plays for the next two hours in the background. My staff knows this is my personal time each morning and they do not bother me with questions. After turning on the music, I make my coffee and sit down at the table with it and the morning newspaper. There are a lot of praise songs on my CDs and as I read, I am also praising and rejoicing. This practice of hearing worship music to start my day has had an amazing impact on the rest of my day.

Scripture Reading

After the paper has been read, it's time to read my Bible. My Bible lays on one of the end tables in the conference room for all to see. I read at least one chapter each morning. I pick different devotional books to read in desiring for God to speak to me in a meaningful way that day. When I read my Bible in the morning like this, I feel God's favor and blessings throughout the day. I meditate on what I read as much as possible throughout the day. I have acquired favorite verses that I have written on 3 x 5 cards and place in my office where I can see them easily. One of my personal favorites is *Jeremiah 29:11,*

> *For I know the plans I have for you, declares the Lord,*
> *not to harm you; plans to give you hope and a future.*

I have this verse on a card by my computer where I see it many times a day. At the end of *Is God's Hand On Your Business?* will be a section with all my favorite verses listed, one for each day of the month. I have a couple of other pictures taped to my desk which convey meaningful messages from God. One is a plant in the center of a bull's eye. The plant is symbolic of growth in my business when I stay right in the very center of the will of God. This is a visual to me that I want to always be right in the center of God's will. I have another small picture of an eagle. This is symbolic of waiting on the Lord, and then mounting up with wings as eagles. God works in His own timing and not ours and we need to be reminded that sometimes we have to wait—to be patient.

Devotional Reading

After reading my Bible, I have a devotional book handy and I read a few pages. I don't usually have time to read a whole chapter, but maybe a section or two. Some of my favorites are Joel Osteen, Beth Moore and Joyce Meyer—there are many Christian inspirational authors who have wonderful spiritual insights to offer. I have been particularly blessed by Joel and Victoria Osteen for the way they encourage, support and lift up. In the next chapter you will read how God used one of Joel's books to further my business in a big way. I also like watching him on TV so I record his service every Sunday and watch it later on. I have heard God speak to me through Joel's messages many times, giving me guidance and encouragement. Daily, I am thankful that his words are in my life.

Prayer

And last, but definitely not least, is a few minutes of prayer. I pray for wisdom and direction, the health and well-being of each of my staff, any pressing needs that are on my mind and that many clients will be served with successful outcomes. I also pray for a hedge of protection around my business, and for internal peace and contentment. But most of all, I pray for God's will to be done, and for His honor and glory to be manifest.

I routinely pray several times a day. I pray when I first wake up in the morning, before even getting out of bed, after my devotional reading, during the day as I seek guidance and the last thing before I go to sleep at night. A great model for prayer was given to us by the Lord's Prayer. Prayer is nothing more than talking to God. He directs us in His word to do this regularly and often. I have been in the habit of praying often and regularly since I was a child and it sustains me. It also brings favor and His hand over my business.

This is my morning routine and has been my practice for over ten years now. I know it is vital to God's hand on Tax Tiger.

There are a few other things I practice that I want to add, because they are also crucial to the success of a Christian business. As time progresses, those things each will be added for the benefit of my staff, my clients and myself. We are a team, a family, and I wouldn't want it any other way.

Church Attendance

Most Christians attend church, but many are very lax about it. To me, it's a must. Christ taught us in His word not to forsake the assembling of ourselves as is the case and the manner for some. It's not an option, it's a command. I know that God blesses when we are faithful in church attendance. I've already described one example of faithfulness in church attendance when I was a teenager in the first chapter, Childhood, and how I was mightily blessed because of it. I go every Sunday morning regardless of where I am, except when I'm traveling and even then, I try to find a church I can attend.

Now I'm not so legalistic that I advocate you must be there every Sunday morning, evening and Wednesday evening

Bible study without fail. Even though that's how I was raised, I believe each person needs to attend as many times a week as God leads, but at least once on Sunday. There is no place I feel closer to the Lord than in His house. I know I reap rewards and favor because of it.

Tithing

This may or may not be a sore spot for some, but I cannot leave out this important command God gives His children if you want His hand on your business. I was fortunate that I was taught this principle of giving as a child. When your father is a Pastor, you learn these things early. I have tithed since I was a child, literally all my life. If I earned a dollar, ten cents would go in the offering plate. It I earned ten dollars, a dollar would go in the plate. The tithe means, a tenth. God commands us to give a tenth of our income back to Him to support His ministry thru the churches. He says, "Will a man rob God?" He takes this principle to the point where if you don't practice it, you are stealing from Him.

This has never been a hard issue for me because I understand the blessings that flow from being obedient. Malachi 3:8-10 states in part,

> … *test me in this, says the Lord Almighty, and see if I will not throw open the floodgates of heaven and pour out so much blessing that you will not have room enough for it.*

If you commit to doing it, there is no struggle. I hear Christians say, "I can't afford it," to which I reply, you can't afford not to. The blessings and favor will come, pressed down and running over. You do your part by being obedient, and God will do His. His promises are true.

The Bible also tells us to give beyond the tithe as much as we can. The tithe should be the minimum we do. I contribute extra to missions. I have a World Vision child that I sponsor each month, I give to the poor and needy, and I give to my father, who now is ministering in Thailand. He moved there several years ago after my mother passed away from cancer. He felt led to devote the last years of his life creating and operating an orphanage for children left to wander the streets with no parents.

Do as God leads and directs you, and you will be blessed.

Volunteer Activities

If there is any time or energy left, and for a lot of you, there may not be, volunteer a little for the Lord's work. In the early years of my business, just getting it off the ground took all the time and energy I had. But now, ten years later, I have a little extra time. So I go once every other week to the jail where I teach a Bible study class to the incarcerated women. That has been one of my greatest projects. I don't preach at them. I share God's and my love through the awesome and wonderful Bible stories.

I love it that many women have come to know the Lord thru this ministry and I am thankful God put it on my heart. It touches my heart that so many women have connected with me and words that I can share through the prison ministry that I've created. Granted, it may be an unlikely activity for me and the work that I do professionally, but has turned into one of the most rewarding things I have done for God. My Bible study time with them has impacted their lives in such a positive way they frequently write me letters. I have included a few in the Appendix at the end of this book. They warm my heart.

Twice a year, I have a small group Bible study in my home for the church. It's a six-week study and that has been a blessing for me to be able to facilitate that project and grow relationships.

I guess I call it, going the extra mile for Jesus. But hear me loud and clear. I don't believe in neglecting family in so doing. There has to be a proper balance in one's life between God, family and work. When I was a child, my father was 100 percent a Pastor and soul-winner. There was little father-child time. I am not shy about saying this, nor do I say it to embarrass him, but only because it is true. The Bible teaches proper balance within the family, and God does not advocate neglecting that balance just to do His work. With that said, I am grateful for the upbringing I had and the knowledge of the Lord which was taught to me.

Marketing

In the early stages of our business, my marketing plan was to imitate what I saw effectively work at the Law Office of Roni Deutch and to run a good commercial on TV. Once it was developed we started running it on various stations across the country. I was so excited to finally see God's plan take action and my first clients calling. Even though the commercial was good, for some unknown reason, it didn't do well. We only had a limited budget for television advertising and it was very expensive. I did not understand why God didn't cause the phones to ring off the hook. I had done everything right.

Marketing I found was so much trial and error. I thought something would work and then it didn't, so ... I'd try something else. Then I thought to keep on trying until it finally worked. There is a science to good marketing but it's hard to analyze and understand.

With only a small budget, we hoped to get it right quickly, but we failed. Some calls resulted from the TV commercial, but nowhere near what was needed. This was discouraging, and I went back to prayer and trusting in Him to provide. I needed something less expensive to bring me leads. As God always provides, He led me to someone who told me I could buy leads from the Internet for 25 cents each. These were names and phone numbers of people who had a tax lien filed in the county recorder's office and thus were public knowledge. Companies compiled those names and sold them!

I thought that was a great deal, so I bought a couple of thousand of them. The problem was they had to be called. This was "cold calling," which I absolutely did not want to do. I did it anyway. I took those names and we started calling. I called for hours every day, even coming in on Saturday to catch people at home. There is nothing harder than cold calling and I hated it. I didn't understand why God was making me take this approach. Why wasn't I successful right away? Well, looking back, He had a lot of things He wanted me to learn. Getting to the top quickly wasn't one of them. I needed to learn patience, and new marketing skills. I needed to struggle to appreciate the journey.

Be Willing To Do What It Takes

And struggle I did. But I did start making sales from all the calls I was doing; enough to pay the bills each month. I committed to doing whatever it took. For two years I worked six days a week and the only day off I had was Sunday. Since I went to church on Sunday, I had very little time to rest. There wasn't a lot of balance in my life in those early years, but my husband was good about it and understood.

I had to be willing to do what it takes. I had to be willing to put in the time, the energy and take the risks. I worked long, hard hours and never took a salary for the first year. My husband had a good job and made enough income for our family, without me bringing home a paycheck. None of us like to struggle or work extra hard, or worry if we will make it, but God's timing is not always our timing, and he teaches us valuable lessons along the way. But you need to be willing and committed to do whatever it takes.

Draw Closer to Him

Struggles and hardships often have the result of drawing us closer to Him. We pray harder, we trust more, we give praise when things go right, and we realize how much we need His help and favor. These early days caused me to draw closer to Him daily. I could feel Him speaking to me through my thoughts. I would have a thought that came into my head all of a sudden—out of the blue. I knew it came from Him. I heard Him speak to me through sermons at church, books I read, scripture, and through people he brought into my path out of the clear blue. Circumstances happened that were totally unexpected. He gave me symbols that had meaning to me from time to time so that I would also remember to trust Him. The symbol I love the most is the rainbow. Rainbows are beautiful beyond description.

On one summer vacation to Hawaii, an environment and state that I love, I was meditating one morning with my cup of coffee on the lanai. I saw the most brilliant rainbow I had ever seen. The colors were distinct and bright. He spoke to me thru my thoughts and said, "This is my sign to you that good things are heading your way. When things look bleak, remember, after the storm always comes the rainbow." I have a painting of one in my office that one of my employees painted for me and it reminds me daily that good things are coming over the horizon.

As I sum up the beginning of Tax Tiger, Inc., I close this chapter with a letter from Carla, my office manager, that she would like to share with you.

Carla Giampapa's Letter

Back in the latter part of 2002, I met a spitfire of a woman named Kathy Hill. Miss Kathy had an idea for a startup company and I joined forces with her to help bring it to fruition. There were constant challenges and we both got our share of bumps and bruises along the way, but we were determined. And ... you have never met a more tenacious person with unshakable faith than Kathy Hill. It is with great pride that I share the following story with you; just one of many, many like it.

As always, Kathy would go into the office several hours early to have quiet prayer time before starting the business day, and I would generally come in about half an hour early to converse with her and plan our day. On one particular occasion, Kathy had let me know of a specific plan/direction she wanted to take for the business. I was thinking to myself how she was nuts to think we could make that plan work. Doing my best to be supportive though (of one of my favorite people), I shared with Kathy that I would follow whatever course she wanted to take, however it would be challenging and perhaps a little far reaching. I just didn't want her to get her hopes up only to be let down. She assured me that she had been praying on it that morning and that was the exact course that we should take. So, I chuckled, knowing her strength of mind, and we went to work. I kid you not, not 20 minutes later, I received a phone call from a random company that had been referred to us and was interested in opening a dialogue about forming an alliance to—get this—accomplish the exact goal that Kathy and I were speaking of earlier that morning. Needless to say, I was beside myself, and, after a brief conversation and taking down the gentleman's information, I hung up the phone and declared to Kathy, "There you go praying' again!" That phrase has turned out to be one of my most used phrases with Kathy. She should be the poster child for "Prayer Works"!

I have now had the pleasure of knowing this amazing woman for ten years and am blessed to have her in my life. Little does Kathy know what a huge influence she has been and continues to be for me. Often times when I'm setting out to accomplish a specific goal and I'm feeling a little insecure, I think to myself, "How would Kathy handle this?" Undoubtedly, the answer always follows: "Pray on it. Then, give thanks knowing that it is done."

Listen to this woman ... You'll learn a lot.

Carla M. Giampapa

7

The Growth Years Continue

The first four years of my Tax Tiger business were the hardest. Everything was trial and error and a complete faith and trust in God. As I look back, I see how important those years were for my instruction and development. God kept me going and continually answered prayer, but I never was able to get very far ahead in profitability. I was able to pay the bills each month, hire a new person every year or so, and stay a debt-free company. A business consultant told me that 90 percent of new businesses fail in the first year. Therefore, I should consider myself blessed. And I was blessed.

The biggest and most impactful (in several ways) blessing came in my fourth year of business. To this day, I will never be able to thank God enough for what happened next.

Let me backtrack just for a minute. Remember my oldest son, David? He had graduated from college years before with a degree in computer animation. His college was in Dallas, Texas. This was in the infancy of the video game business and he was snapped up by a large video game company to develop new games. It paid great money and although I was disappointed he wasn't coming back to California, I was happy for him. He is extremely talented and smart and did well working for this company for several years. The tiger logo he designed for me turned out to be hugely popular and successful in helping to brand the company name. He and his wife had just had a new baby girl and he had taken several weeks off to be at home.

During this same period of time, my office manager, Carla, shocked me one day and announced she was giving me notice. She had come from a background of movie production and wanted to go back to it. Honestly, I was devastated. Carla had brought our business from a total start-up to a functioning and fairly successful, operating business. I knew I could never make it without her and was very upset. Carla was not a Christian during her years of employment with us, but I tried at every opportunity to witness to her of God's love and grace. On a regular basis, she did witness God's answers to my prayers and would comment often that I must have a direct line to heaven.

There were times when a payroll was due on a specific day and I would tell her that I would have to go to prayer and God would provide. I would always make a sale with just enough money to meet the need that day before the end of the day. She was always amazed when this happened.

Carla didn't abruptly leave. She gave me a couple months notice and encouraged me by saying that everything would be fine, and I would be able to find someone just as good as she had been. I was still extremely doubtful and very upset. My faith didn't quite stand up to the test this time. I forgot to trust. Sometimes when major disappointment strikes, we fall short of our faith. Even though my trust fell short, my prayers didn't. I once again took it to the Lord.

Then the most amazing and wonderful thing happened. While David was on family leave, he was laid off from his job. They were experiencing problems and had laid off one round of employees already. He was laid off on the second round. And he was naturally devastated. With a wife and new baby, this was not a good thing. He tried unsuccessfully to find a new job.

On the day that Carla gave me notice, I was sitting at my desk in tears and I called David to tell him what had happened. After I told him Carla was leaving, there was a very long pause on the phone. He always had been my encourager and supporter and never let me down. He listened. And then he said, "Well, Mom, I think I would like to apply for that position." I was shocked. I said, "Seriously?" He said he had wanted to get back to California. I told him there was no way I could pay him what he was used to making and he said that was OK because if he helped me build the business, and his wife worked, they could make it until I could afford a raise for him.

As ecstatic as I was, I raised a doubt. He had no background in accounting or knowing the QuickBooks software. He had no experience running a company, (but then neither did I) and that worried me a little. So when I voiced that reservation, he said simply, "I can learn."

Think about that for a minute. Here I had been willing for years to allow God to teach me new things and I had been learning a lot, and my son says to me, "I can learn." I offered to fly him out to California for a week and asked him to sit by Carla's side and observe and tell me at the end of the week if he thought he could do it.

After watching her for two days, he told me, "I can do this." Wow!!!! Oh, the wonder of God's plan for us. My favorite business verse is Jeremiah 29:11. It tells us of the plans God has to prosper us, to give us hope and a future. Who would have thought that David would have been laid off at the same time that Carla gave me notice? That is not coincidence! It is God's favor shining down in a very big way. This incident is one of many where God used unexpected circumstances out of the blue to promote growth in our business and in a big way.

"I have good things on the horizon for you and am sending you this rainbow so that each time you see one, it will remind you of my favor and great plans I have for you. Also, after every challenge or disappointment you go through, there will be a rainbow waiting."

Symbols

God also used symbols throughout the years to give me strength and hope from time to time. I knew they had meaning and were from Him because I felt it in my spirit when they occurred. The rainbow is one of the most special to me.

One morning in Hawaii, as I was finishing my morning devotional time, sitting on the lanai with a cup of coffee and my Bible, I looked up and beheld the most beautiful rainbow I have ever seen. It was brilliant and unlike any other. The colors were distinct and did not overlap into each other as they usually do. It traversed a complete half circle starting in the beautiful green hills of Kauai and ending in the ocean of Hanalei Bay. I had just finished praying and was meditating on God's word. The sudden appearance of this rainbow was a direct message to me.

The thought that came into my mind from Him was, "I have good things on the horizon for you and am sending you this rainbow so that each time you see one, it will remind you of my favor and great plans I have for you. Also, after every challenge or disappointment you go through, there will be a rainbow waiting." Those words were clear and meaningful to me, and I recognized God was speaking them directly to me.

In the years since, every time I see a rainbow, I hear those same words from the Lord and it gives me strength and a greater measure of faith each time. The painting in my office, the one that a staff member painted for me when she heard me speak about the rainbow experience, is a constant reminder. I will forever see that one particular rainbow in my mind's eye.

Unfortunately, when the phone books were delivered to our home, he looked up our ad to see how it looked ... and then he noticed the fish....

I have spoken briefly of other symbols that God has given me to provide extra strength and faith for me. Another one is the eagle. The Word of God tells us that we can mount up as an eagle if we will but wait on Him. One summer I was at our cabin in the mountains which sits right on the banks of a small creek with rushing water. I love the mountains almost as much as I love the beauty of Hawaii. As I sat on a big rock one afternoon overlooking the creek, I heard a rushing noise and looked up. There, just a little ways above my head, was a majestic eagle flying up river. It was an awesome sight. God spoke to me and said, "See, if you continue to follow me and wait on me, I will make you and your company soar like the eagle. I have never forgotten that amazing sight, and have the picture of an eagle taped to my desk to remind me of His promise in Psalm 103:5: "Who satisfies your desires with good things so that your youth is renewed like the eagle's."

I have another symbol of a plant and a bull's eye target; it symbolizes staying in the center of God's will. This is critical to me, because unless you strive daily to be in the center of His will, you will stray off course and the favor and blessings will not come in the fullness they would otherwise. This is not an easy thing to do because sometimes you just don't know what His will is. He tells us to seek it, and it, we will find; to continually pray for it and He will show it to us. Pray daily for God to show you His will and to keep you right smack in the center of it. This is my prayer each morning.

Then I have a symbol that you will all recognize, the Footprints in the Sand message. You can find these words on everything nowadays, but when our business was very young, my youngest son, John Paul, gave me as a Christmas gift one year a Footprints in the Sand plaque which had footprints carved in the beautiful piece of wood. I loved it and again God spoke to me. He said when I was weary and felt I couldn't go

Tax Tiger logo

Kathy with white tiger: Tigers for Taxpayers.

Reception desk.

Comfort comes first.

A comfortable lakeside view.

Creative Marketing.

My sons David and John Paul.

Sitting on deck outside my office.

Symbols That Touch My Soul

*But they that wait upon the Lord
shall renew their strength;
they shall mount up with wings as eagles;
they shall run, and not be weary;
and they shall walk, and not faint.*

Isaiah 40:31 KJV

When you wait, you soar.

Scripture Card

*"For I know the plans I have for you
declares the Lord, plans to prosper
you and not to harm you; plans to
give you hope and a future."*

NIV Jeremiah 29:11

God's promise.

Footprints in the Sand

One night I dreamed I was walking along the beach with the lord.
Many scenes from my life flashed across the sky.
In each scene I noticed footprints in the sand.
Sometimes there were two sets of footprints,
other times there was one set of footprints.

This bothered me because I noticed
that during the low periods of my life,
when I was suffering from anguish, sorrow or defeat,
I could see only one set of footprints.

So, I said to the lord, "You promised me Lord,
that if I followed you, you would walk with me always.
But I have noticed that during the most trying periods in my life
there have only been one set of footprints in the sand.
Why, when I needed you most, have you not been there for me?"

The Lord replied,
"The times when you only have seen one set of footprints in the sand,
is when I carried you."

When the struggles get too much to carry, He will carry you.

God's promise of blessings after a storm.

Deflecting Satan

*"Put on the whole armor of God,
that you may be able to stand
against the wiles of the devil."*

NIV Ephesians 6:11

Resisting Satan.

Growing in the center of God's will.

on, He would carry me. I love that message and although the plaque hangs in my living room, he also gave me a beautiful dish the next year with the same symbol which sits in my office. There have been times when I prayed, "OK Lord, you're gonna need to carry me a bit."

Lastly, and just as important to my business, is the symbol of the fish. This is the universal symbol of Christianity. There are many businesses that use this symbol in their advertising to glorify God and identify themselves to the public. I believe it is crucially important in your business to take a stand for the One who stands for you. Sadly, it was this issue that pretty much drove the final wedge into my marriage.

The following year that David took over the position of Director of Operations at Tax Tiger, he was developing our advertising in the yellow pages and decided to use the symbol of the fish in the ad. I'm sorry to say that it wasn't my idea, but I supported his ad none the less. I knew, however, when I saw the proof, that my husband would have a fit, and I dreaded the confrontation that was sure to come. He was adamant about keeping Christ out of the business.

Now mind you, he never worked there for one single day. He had another job and it was, from day one, my business to operate. Because he owned it with me, he felt he had a say in this as well as in many other things. (The startup loan was repaid within two years.) Yes, he did have a say—he was my partner. But, this is further evidence of what happens when you are unequally yoked, both in marriage and business. There is no compatibility or common ground in spiritual areas.

Nevertheless, my faith was more important, so I authorized the ad. I took the proof home one evening to show him. I waited for the explosion to come, but amazingly, he glanced at it and never noticed the sign of the fish at the bottom corner of the ad. I couldn't believe it, but sure as the world, I wasn't going to point it out. The ad was printed in the phone book, which is good for one year before reprinting. Unfortunately, when the phone books were delivered to our home, he went to our ad to see how it looked and then he noticed the fish. He exploded on me and was extremely angry. I reminded him that I had showed him the proof, but he was not appeased. There was also nothing he could do as the ad was already in print. But my marriage took a definite turn for the worse.

The final nail in the coffin of marital strife came when he overheard me talking about how I had prayed with a client on the phone who was in distress over IRS issues. He ordered me to never talk about God in the workplace as it was inappropriate. I stood my ground and stated that over half my staff was Christian and we did talk about God on a daily basis and would continue to do so and he would not order me to refrain, particularly since he didn't even work there. He had an explosive temper when he got angry and said some very hateful and hurtful things to me. The next day when I got home from work the phone book was open to divorce attorneys. He had called around while I was at work. We ended up arriving at a truce of sorts after the arguments died down but frankly, I no longer cared.

The marriage lasted for another two years, but it was basically, for both of us, now an empty relationship. I paid a heavy price to go against God's will and engage in disobedience. Thankfully, God never gave up on me; he continued to show me rainbows, eagles and footprints in the sand.

Progress

When David came to Tax Tiger, there was immediate and significant progress in many areas. The biggest was in the area of marketing. Any business knows that strategic and well-thought-out marketing is the key to success. My marketing up to that point was sorely lacking expertise. I had tried the TV commercials which had made Roni Deutch millions. That didn't work for me so I tried buying lien lists that were very inexpensive. The Lord led me to this form of marketing through a conversation I heard from a person at another company.

There were companies on line who compiled lists of individuals who owed the IRS and had a lien placed on their home with the County Recorder's Office. My excitement quickly dimmed, however; very few people were home and we mostly got answering machines. I devised a great message to leave on their machine and waited for the call backs. Few returned the calls. I decided that most were at work during the day and unless I was able to reach them to actually speak with them, it was going to be difficult. I did get just enough call backs to keep the bills paid. God provided just enough but not much extra.

I decided in order to get the maximum number of people to speak with personally, I needed to work on Saturday when people would likely be home. I did reach more people, and sales picked up. My people skills of earlier years that the Lord developed in me—my rapport and sales capability—were now being put to use in a big way. For two solid years I worked on Saturday. I never had a day off except for Sunday, and because I went to church, I only had a half a day or so of personal and family time. It was hard. But I kept on. There was a commitment level in my heart that never wavered. I continued to make sales.

God then led me to a marketing expert who advised me to do a direct mail campaign with all those names I had purchased. It was an "old-fashioned" technique, but he thought I should be able to reach more of them than I had done up to this point. I tried that next. Direct mail historically has a very low rate of return, but is relatively inexpensive to maintain. I got more sales from that but still not enough to meet my goals.

When David came, he took my marketing into the 21st century. He knew the most effective way was the Internet. I had no clue about Internet marketing. He learned the ins and outs of pay-per-click advertising. We started Internet marketing, and it was highly successful! It was the perfect outreach to our prospective clientele. This means that when a person has tax problems, they will most likely search the Internet for help. What key word they type in to find that help is crucial in finding a company. We developed hundreds of key words that people might use to lead them to our website.

David also redesigned our Tax Tiger website to make it more effective. However, Internet marketing is a science in and of itself. Effective advertising on the Internet was still a struggle, relatively speaking, as many of our competitors used the same type of marketing. The key: the more you were willing to spend for a particular key word would determine how high up in the rankings you would reach and how soon people could find you. David did a magnificent job in this area and I will be forever grateful to him for taking us to a whole new level.

Tax Tiger expanded and grew by:

- Diversifying our marketing into other areas. God gave us an unexpected blessing one day when we got a call from a yellow page ad company. They had two openings for tax resolution companies to promote and they chose us as one of the two because of our stellar reputation, which has always been an A+ with the Better Business Bureau. We got millions of dollars of yellow page advertising nationally for terms that were unbelievable. We have carried that contract to this day and it has given us many clients for very little cost.

- Hiring a Christian business consultant to advise us and meet with him on a semi-monthly basis. He gave us valuable guidance and wisdom for several years.

- Advertising was important. David and I designed a new TV commercial and flew to LA to film it. It was low budget, but turned out very well and still plays today on TV and is on my website. It generated some good business, but TV ads continue to be very expensive and we still are limited as to how much we can afford.

- Creating awesome radio spots and giving radio a try. They worked well on occasion depending on where we ran them. The Sirius ad we currently run is a home run in terms of successful radio advertising.

- Actively soliciting referrals from tax firms who do not want to do this kind of tax resolution strengthened our visibility and success. We get many referrals and grateful clients from them.

Tax Tiger was now diversified and even though we still strive to do better in a highly competitive industry, God has blessed us beyond my greatest desires. The turning point was the incredible gift of having my son on staff with me and being able to work with him on a daily basis. God is so good!

With the company now experiencing good growth, along with it came the need for additional staff and additional office space. The staff part was another God story because many of them simply came to me at the exact time I needed them, literally walking in the door on a given day.

When I needed to add one more financial analyst (sales person), one day in walked one of my dearest friends and asked if I had any openings. He was from back in my network marketing days; someone who I hadn't seen since I started Tax Tiger. His name was Anthony, and he was one of the best sales people I had ever known. His skill and abilities have blessed my company with success, for over six years now, and I would not have the number of clients I do now without him. Needless to say, he didn't have to ask twice. Friends, do you see how God used my past experiences to bless me down the road in the future? This happened over and over again.

I asked for guidance. I listened. I responded.

One day a man walked through the Tax Tiger doors without an appointment, asking to see me. He had heard of Tax Tiger from an attorney friend who had worked for Roni Deutch. He was an enrolled agent (a specialist in tax resolution and tax preparation) and wondered if I had any job openings. It was at a time when I was about a month away from needing another person and he "fit the bill." (Anthony, my sales director, is still with me to this day.)

Another time when I needed a new case worker, a CPA faxed over a resume out of the blue. I interviewed him and hired him immediately. He was young, bright, and aggressive with the IRS.

An e-mail was received from a young lady I had met at a conference; she worked at a very large company and with one of my competitors. We had met over dinner one night because I was friendly with the owner of this firm. A year later, she asked for an appointment to see me for a position. She would be moving to Sacramento in a few months and would love to work for me. She has turned out to be an awesome employee and a huge blessing. She remains with me to this day.

On the rare occasion when I needed a receptionist or an administrative position, and placed an ad on Craig's list, I got over a hundred resumes in a few hours and had to weed through them. Staffing, as a result, has never been an issue for me, for the most part. Most have been with me for long periods of time, six years or so, but recognizing how critical good staff is, I pray earnestly for the right person when I do need to add someone.

The need for increased office space was much harder to deal with. I have previously described how beautiful and awesome my office space is and how God gave it to me. But what he gave me in the beginning only had room enough for five offices and a conference room. There are three small office buildings on this little lake and all of the tenants had been there for years. No additional space ever "came up for grabs." This was and is prime office space on the water. When I needed to add more staff, there was nowhere to expand.

One day, out of desperation, I toured the building where my space was located and asked the other office-holders if their lease was up for renewal anytime soon and would they be renewing. I found the woman across the hall had an office with two rooms and her lease would be up in a couple of months. She lived quite a distance from the office and drove over 30 minutes to work every day, but she probably would renew for one more year. I called the property manager and said I would be willing to sign a five year lease on that space if I could have it. Since the other woman wouldn't sign for five years, I got the space. Every space I picked up, including my original space, I went out on a limb for—as I always did. I took a risk ... and signed for five years.

A year later, the office next door came up for renewal and I did the same thing. I offered a five year lease and because the transportation company next door wouldn't match it, I got that space. That was four more spaces. That worked for a while until a couple years later, when I picked up two more spaces down the hall.

The most amazing God story here regarding office space though, is when the State Farm agent, who had three offices in the next building, and had been there for almost twenty years, decided to move to Texas. When this happened, it was at a time when I didn't need more space. Now I had a dilemma. If I didn't take it, someone else would and quickly. David and I conferred. He did not want to incur the extra cost. Neither did my husband, who, not unexpectedly, also said an empathic no.

Those of faith often refer to a "Higher Power." I was no different. Yes, David was an important component of the growing Tax Tiger. And at this time, my husband was still legally my husband and partner in the business, but we didn't share the same vision—neither for the business nor for our lives. I knew in my heart that it was time to deal decisively with both very soon.

I turned to my other partner. I didn't want unnecessary cost either, but the Lord seemed to be speaking to me that I would need it one day. As I am a visionary and try to think ahead to the future a little, I devoted a lot of prayer to it. I asked for guidance. I listened. I responded.

Against both of their wishes, I took the extra space. It was one of the few times David and I have disagreed on a business decision. It turned out to be the right decision and within a few weeks I needed the space. I signed another five year lease. You have to step out in faith and believe that God will provide when you feel Him leading you. Yes, it involves risk. **But where God guides, he provides.**

The many varied and marvelous ways His hand was on my business and guiding each step has been wonderful for me to behold. How grateful I am that He is my partner and guides my ship.

8

My Vision

Tax Tiger was now at the point where we were a successful, thriving company. The thousands of clients we touched saw amazing and spectacular results in their lives. In the Appendix, I've included a few that have shared letters so you can see the difference we made and are continuing to make in people's lives. But let me share at least one with you now.

Mary Smith's Letter

Finding Tax Tiger was an answer to my prayers. I had an IRS tax liability of $57,000, and had searched for months for a reputable organization to help me. I had not been able to work for two years due to illness and I was too overwhelmed to even attempt a research process for much of that time. Every company I found on the Internet seemed questionable to me. Those I actually contacted gave me no confidence that they really cared or would have my best interest. Finally, I put out a very clear intention that I would only work with a company with high integrity and with people who were genuine and caring ... even though I didn't really believe such a company existed!

And then, I found Tax Tiger,

There were two things that immediately got my attention: they are a faith-based organization and they have an A+ Better Business Bureau rating. I was deeply moved by the Founder and CEO's story of deciding to found an ethical tax resolution company after observing firsthand the poor treatment of clients in her employment with another agency. When I contacted Tax Tiger I knew I had found my team. I was scared and overwhelmed with my debt. They were nothing but compassionate, kind and professional. Every single person who dealt directly with me on my case was an advocate for me, walking me through the steps with a calming and reassuring presence. They have treated me with incredible kindness and respect.

As a former business owner, I know what to pay attention to when evaluating a company for its integrity and client care. And their rates are amazingly fair and straightforward. There's nothing hidden.

Tax Tiger is a stellar organization in every way: They are an A+++++++ company, and the best part, they negotiated my debt of $57,000 down to $837! It's hard to believe there's a better tax resolution company in the country.

There are no adequate words to fully express how grateful I am to have found Tax Tiger. If you want to cut to the chase and avoid agonizing wasted time looking at other tax resolution companies, go directly to Tax Tiger first. They're truly the real deal.

Mary Smith
Mill Valley, CA

How could I reach out to more? How could I help the many who were at their wits end? How could I help those who were being misled on their rights and remedies?

Our office space was at capacity and there was no more room for additional staff. Yet, I still felt we could do better. I wanted to have a bigger national presence and recognition, not for the glory and fame, but because so many thousands of taxpayers continued to get ripped off by not only the big three mega firms, but many others as well. To my dismay, there are taxpayer predators everywhere. On a daily basis, my offices get calls from taxpayers with stories of spending $9000 to $10,000 with other companies, only to have nothing done for them. Their calls are laced with tears and depression— my staff senses that we are their last hope. I gave small discounts as best I could but they had to repay for services all over again. I only wish somehow I could help them all. Each year, I do a small number of pro bono cases. Their situations, to me, are heart-breaking ... and unnecessary.

How could I reach out to more? How could I help the many who were at their wits end? How could I help those who were being misled on their rights and remedies?

As I pondered on how to grow a bigger national presence, even though we now had clients in almost all of the 50 states, I didn't see an answer. I did not want to move to another building with more room because God gave me the one I had—plus it was perfect for me. There was no more room to expand, no one else to give up any room and we were using every nook and cranny that we had. Other space in the building was non-existent—all the other tenants were there to stay.

It was during the summer and we had gone to our cabin in the mountains for a week's vacation. Dick had inherited a wonderful, rustic and beautiful (to me) cabin from his folks when we got married. It was a gift to him for us and was enjoyed by us for many years. We went there during all of our dating years and during our marriage every chance we could. The cabin was very close to Lake Almanor in Northern California and sat on the banks of the Feather River, which ran behind it. We had a shared love of the mountains. He loved fishing and tried to teach me. I just didn't have the patience, and my fingernails kept getting in the way. I did however, learn to clean a fish. That should earn me some points, for you men who are reading *Tax Tiger*.

He would fish, and I would sit on the bank, between some beautiful pine trees in the forest and read a good book. I would cheer whenever he caught one. Yes, I tried very hard to be a good wife in spite of our many differences.

Let me interject here that even though I have described our spiritual incompatibility, there were a lot of good times and happy moments during our marriage and our dating years. We had many memorable moments which we laugh about to this day, even though we are now divorced.

As I write this, I remember the time we had gone down to the Sacramento River one afternoon for a drive. Dick pulled off the main road, drove down into some tall grass beside the river and parked in some soft sand. We got out and walked along the river a bit. When we got back in the truck to leave, the wheels started to spin. The soft sand created no traction. He was very upset and didn't know what to do, adding that he was worried the hot engine would catch the grass on fire.

OK, people, forgive me, but now I have to brag just a bit. I knew exactly what to do. I, the girl who could do numbers and deal with the IRS, had a mechanical trick up her sleeves. I ran down to the river and searched for several of the flattest rocks I could find. Gathering them up, I brought them back and got down on my hands and knees by the truck. He watched with an amused look on his face. I dug out a deep well with my bare hands under each of the back tires, and wedged those flat rocks in as far as I could under each tire.

With disbelief written all over him, and yet, the amused look still in his eyes, I told him to get in the truck and hit the gas. Sure enough, the truck drove right out on top of those rocks. Hooray and thumbs up for me! Smile!

He later laughed when he told that story to his friends about how I dug his truck out and how I looked like a puppy dog down on my hands and knees digging in the dirt. His friends all laughed, pointed at me, and said, "She's a keeper."

I'm the first to admit it; I also had my own share of faults so I in no way want to imply that our marriage failure was his entire fault. We did have good times, and shared experiences that were meaningful and significant.

Anyway, back to our summer vacation at the cabin. I had a habit of walking through the forest each morning when I woke up with my cup of coffee and used that time to pray and meditate. There was a path that ran amongst the trees behind the cabins in a circular route. It was lovely and beautiful. About half way around, there was a big tree stump that I would choose to sit down on and pray. I did this each morning.

Being a morning person, I was up by 6:30; he could easily sleep until mid-morning starting his day with brunch. There was no way that I could just lay there for several hours waiting for him to wake up, an issue that always hung between us and actually increased over the years we were together. On multiple occasions, he had told me he resented me getting up before him. It was one of those gnats that became an elephant in the room over time. Some things you just have to deal with and that was one of them.

This particular morning as I sat on the stump, my heart and mind were striving to find God's plan for any further business expansion. I prayed about it and asked Him to show me what to do. I told God that I would do whatever He led me to do as I wanted to be in the center of His will, even if it meant that this was as far as we could go.

Listening to God

I will never forget what happened next. As I sat there meditating after my prayer time, one word popped into my head, "franchise." It was as clear as a bell. It caught me up short. I said out loud, "Lord, did you say franchise? I don't know the first thing about franchising." The response that vibrated through my head and my very being was clear and direct, "You can learn." A little stunned, I felt that there was an echo. This was exactly what my son David had said to me, "I can learn." Wow!!!! Really? I can learn? Seriously? How many new things must I continue to learn?

This was visionary and pioneering.
It had never been done.
Could it be done? God said so ...

Hearing and listening to God's voice have been critical factors in my survival through the rough times and my success. Let me say a few things about listening, really listening, and hearing, really hearing, God's voice. I don't believe God speaks in actual words or sounds that we can hear with our human ears. He speaks through our thoughts and in the quiet times of our spirit and hearts. If we pray and are open and ready to hear, he will answer us. And He will speak to us. He answers in His own timing and in His own will and way, and whether it's yes or no, or wait a little, he answers. We need to be attuned to listening for these words that come into our minds totally unannounced and unexpectedly. I am tuned to listening for Him and have been for many years. I know when the thoughts I have are from Him. You will too.

When I heard the word "franchise," I knew of many of the franchises we see every day: McDonald's, Taco Bell, and my favorite (because the CEO is a hero of mine) Chick Fil A, etc. In my industry of tax resolution, there had never been such a thing as a franchise. This was visionary and pioneering. It had never been done. Could it? God said so, so I was determined to find out.

I got back to the cabin and picked up my daily devotional book that I happened to be reading at the time. It was one of Joel Osteen's books, *Become a Better You.* As I mentioned earlier, Joel Osteen happens to be one of my favorite ministers, and God has used him many, many times to give me encouragement, guidance and courage to follow through. I was deep into the second chapter, "Give Your Dreams a New Beginning."

As I picked it up, I read,

God is saying this is a time of new beginnings.... Keep pressing forward and keep believing. You've got the gifts, the talents, and the dreams. Don't allow complacency to keep you from seeing God's promises fulfilled in your life.

This seemed further confirmation to me of what God had just said, even though the idea seemed way too big for me. Then I read in I Chronicles 4:10, "... Oh, that you would bless me and enlarge my territory! Let your hand be with me, and keep me from harm so that I will be free from pain. And God granted his request."

When I got home, I began a search online in order to learn about franchising. I found it was an extremely complex process. It involved putting together complicated legal documents and an operations manual. I hadn't the slightest idea of the difficulty or expense in trying to achieve this huge undertaking. After more research, I found some expert franchise consultants from North Carolina who had been doing this for over 20 years. After speaking with them by phone, I learned they would come to my business, look it over and evaluate the potential of franchising. I told them they would need to come at their own expense. They agreed and we made a date.

Bob and Lizette Pirtle flew to Sacramento and spent a day at Tax Tiger with us, looking at the entire operation and asking a lot of questions. At the end of the day, they looked at me and said,

> We have franchised a lot of businesses over the years, but we have never seen anything as amazing as what we've seen here today. What you do for people is the most touching and meaningful thing we have ever seen. You make a huge difference in people's lives. We believe this is a tremendous opportunity for you to franchise what you have achieved here at Tax Tiger.

To say that I was surprised at the high praise from a very experienced couple who did this for a living would be an understatement. Every business owner wants kudos, let's face it. I wondered, "Did they say this to everyone?" Their genuine, heartfelt comments, however, assured me this was real for them and unusual.

I then asked the inevitable, "What did their services cost?"

That's when the sticker shock came in. They said $100,000 and about a year of time would be needed to complete the project. I almost fell over. I didn't have a hundred thousand dollars sitting around—what small business has that much ready cash available? As they left, I said I would be in touch. Oh boy, where was I going to get that type of money—this wasn't just a few thousand dollars—this was ONE HUNDRED THOUSAND DOLLARS! Where would it come from? Who could guide me in seeking a source? Of course, the answer was within my grasp. I knew it well. Once again, I went to the Lord in prayer, my trusted ally and confidant. I told Him that it was just too much for me to try and deal with but if it was His will, He would need to provide the means.

Surprisingly, my husband was supportive of the idea, but was skeptical of raising the money. The only way I knew how to do this was to try for a loan at my bank, Wells Fargo—the traditional way, and a way where small businesses had experienced not only doors firmly closing on them—doors were slamming in their faces. This was a critical time in our country right then. The economy was failing, businesses were failing right and left, and banks were refusing to loan any money at all. It was all over the nightly news. I remember hearing that a business had been turned down for a loan of $5,000. There simply was no money out there. It was a dire time in our economy. I knew there was no chance in the world that we would be able to get any kind of a loan, but I would go through the motions if it was what God wanted me to do. Here again, my faith got a little weak. I'm not perfect in my walk with my Lord, but I try hard.

I called my Wells Fargo where we had banked for six years. They had my banking history from day one. Two loan officers came out to my office and brought loan papers to fill out. They asked what I wanted the loan for and how this would work. I explained my plan and what my consultants had told us. They took the application and said they would give me a decision in a week or so.

A week later they came back out with their decision. They sat down at my conference room table with us and I prepared myself for the rejection. They looked at me and said they had reviewed the plan, my track record of business for the past six years, the fact we were a debt free company, and had decided to approve the loan of $100,000. My mouth dropped open. Further, they said they had decided to give me an additional $100,000 line of credit and a $25,000 company credit card, neither of which I had asked for. The tears streamed down my face and I was totally overwhelmed. They said I wouldn't need to commence repaying the loan for nine months to give me time to develop the program, and then it would be a four-year loan at a very low interest rate.

Here again, my faith got a little weak. I'm not perfect in my walk with my Lord, but I try hard.

I had never felt God's hand on my business more closely than at that moment. It was a miracle. It was His favor. It was His plan for me after all. Even now, more than four years later, I have a hard time telling that story without the tears. I told them I didn't need a line of credit. They said I might one day and I should have it just in case. Oh, the mighty wonder of God's plans for His children who strive to stay in His will and be obedient when He asks the hard things.

That started a long, and arduous process of both legal development and getting it all planned out. Bob and Lizette flew once a month to Sacramento to meet with us for a week at a time for planning and development sessions. They had a business relationship with a major franchise law firm in Denver, Colorado, who began putting the FDD (the legal document) together. We had to put every single thing in our operations, down to the smallest detail, onto paper to be designed into an operations manual. That was very hard and took a year to accomplish. But the premise of a franchise is that the person buying one will be able to follow the manual and be able to hit the ground running from day one.

It was finally almost ready to be made public. I wasn't sure how to market this opportunity and had a small nagging fear of getting the wrong franchisee in who would ruin my stellar reputation. I knew I needed to be very careful and interview prospects thoroughly and investigate companies who would market my franchise opportunity. They all wanted a lot of money. Lots.

My option now was obvious. I needed to take on this task myself. I sent letters out to all the CPA firms around the country explaining the opportunity. I began to get a few calls and letters back. It was my general goal to appoint around 20 franchises throughout the United States, covering every one of the four time zones, and some of the major cities, but not so many as to dilute the profitability for all of us—just enough to collectively be a national force to be reckoned with. I want many more hurting taxpayers to see us and call us before calling any one among the number of disreputable companies out there. This is my vision.

Franchise #1

How my very first franchise came into being is another one of God's greatest gifts to me. When I was in the development stages, I was talking one evening on the phone with my youngest son, John Paul, who now lived in Texas. He had graduated from college a couple of years before with two business degrees and had gone into the field of financial planning and real estate. He had married a wonderful girl who was in some of his college classes and who majored in accounting and was going to get her CPA license. They moved from Idaho where they both had graduated, to Austin, Texas. They chose Austin because the cost of living was lower there than in California and because it is a thriving and progressive city.

He had been trying very hard to get a foothold into financial planning but that wasn't working well for him. So, if the economy was in a nose dive and banks weren't loaning money, and 401ks were losing money, why would there be much of a market there? It was the same way with real estate. God was closing doors for him and guiding him in a different direction.

As we spoke on the phone that night, we were chatting about life in general and I began to tell him about my new vision for franchising Tax Tiger. I was excited about it and was sharing some of the planning. There was a long pause on the phone; just as there had been with David on that day some years back; and he finally said, "I think I might like to buy one of your franchises." I was floored. Never in my wildest dreams would I have ever thought John Paul would want to join me in my business. He said he had watched me grow my business for years and would love to be the "pilot" franchise to prove it could work for anyone.

Let me digress for a moment. John Paul had always had an entrepreneurial spirit like mine. When in college, he bought an apartment building close to the school as well as several homes and rented them out to college students and made money. Before he went to college, he did some years in the Marines after which he worked his way up from a checker in a grocery store to the store manager where he increased the store profit by a considerable margin. He had a bright mind and a "can do" attitude. Both my sons are extremely smart and I am blessed. However, John Paul had no knowledge of the tax resolution industry.

When I pointed out that he was not an Enrolled Agent, he gave me the same, "I can learn," comment I had heard from his brother. By this time, whenever that comment was made, I was on board.

He said he would begin immediately to study for the Enrolled Agent Test which comes in three parts and is very hard. You must pass them all to get your license to practice tax before the IRS. He completed the necessary studies, took the tests, passed them all the first time and in less than two months, became an Enrolled Agent. I was very proud of him. I sold the first franchise to him, and knew that if he could do it with no experience, just by following the operations manual and training with my office, then anyone could do it. At least anyone with desire, some commitment to learning, and some reasonable business ability could do it.

When the program was ready to roll out and all the legal paperwork in place, John Paul went through some training with me and then I flew to Austin and helped him set up an office. He got a beautiful office space rent-free for six months—something you can do with commercial real estate space in today's economy. Thankfully, he did not have the same difficult learning curve that I did, but worked hard for almost a year with only one other employee, a receptionist. John Paul used my sales staff in the beginning to do his sales for him. He grew by leaps and bounds and to this day has the most successful franchise of all of them and makes a tremendous amount of money. Praise God! I now had both my brilliant and wonderful sons working with me and I would never have imagined it. God's hand is truly on my business!

Franchise #2

My second franchise—this one in San Diego—is clearly another God story. I have so many God stories that I marvel over God's favor and goodness daily. Let me pave the way for you a bit.

What they were missing was the fact that these people were actually excellent credit risks....

Several years before my franchising vision, I had been searching for a finance company to finance my clients' fees to me. I was tired of sending out hundreds of statements every month, then calling clients when their payments were late and having to spread out our fee over twelve months in order to get paid. I had been searching for a finance company for over a year. I talked to many without success but no one would touch my clients. The vast majority of them were bad credit risks and had tax liens. There apparently was no recourse.

As strenuously as I argued for them to think outside the box and give us a chance, no one would even consider it. What they were missing was the fact that these people were actually excellent credit risks because we were doing something they desperately needed; getting the IRS off their backs and settling the debt. If they defaulted on a payment, we would stop work on their case, so they were motivated to make the payments each month and they clearly understood the work would stop if they defaulted.

I had prayed about it earnestly, but the right company never surfaced, until one day, a stranger referred me to a finance company down in San Diego. He thought they might be willing to listen. I called them and got an account manager on the phone. He heard me out and said no. Oh man, here we go again. But one of my personality characteristics that

God has given me is persistence. I just kept on arguing with him to think outside the box and take it to his management for some discussion. Finally, there was a long pause on the phone (whenever I hear these long pauses, I now am prepared to expect good things are about to happen).

After the long pause, he said it was an interesting proposal and he would get back to me. He called back some days later asking questions about my default rate. I told him I had an exceedingly low default rate. After all, who is going to default when I am taking $50,000 of IRS debt and settling it for $50? He said that he had managed to get approval to bring the Director of Accounts and himself to visit my office and get a better picture of our company. He came one day and brought Mike Call with him. Mike was the corporate management executive who ultimately would investigate the company and recommend approval—or not. Mike and his partner spent a whole day with David and me. We gave them all our numbers and showed them the business, which they did not have a clear understanding of at all.

At the end of the day, they both said they were extremely impressed with what they had seen and the difference we were making in so many lives. They said they had never seen a company like ours. They were going to present what they had found to the president of the company and get back to me. Several days later, Mike called to tell me we had been approved. This was huge for me. Someone was finally willing to take a chance on us. They would bill my clients each month, collect the money and remit to me for a small fee. That took a huge load off my staff. They also agreed to buy half of my accounts right up front, which now gave me better cash flow.

This relationship lasted for four years and turned out to be beneficial for both of us. When the franchising planning got under way, I had a creative thought and decided to call up Sean, the account manager to ask him one question: if I brought several franchisees to the table, could I get a small override on that additional business?

One of my traits is that I'm always looking for ways to do better. When I placed the call that morning, the receptionist told me that Sean was in a meeting with Mike and the company President. She said she would put me through to them. I said absolutely not, as I didn't want to interrupt a management meeting. She ignored my objection, said, "No problem" and put me right into the President's office. I was mortified as I didn't want to just blurt out my idea to all three of them together.

God has reasons for the way things happen. Taking a deep breath, I told them about my new franchising plans and asked my question. The President said he would consider my request and let me know how much they could give me, if anything. Hanging up the phone, I went on to my other work.

I had only been off the phone a few minutes when it rang. It was Mike, calling me back from his own office. He asked me a few questions about the franchise plan and then there was a long pause. I knew something was going to pour out from the other end of the line; I just wasn't sure what it was. Yeah, you're getting the picture here. After the pause, he said, "I think I might be interested in buying a franchise. I have wanted to own my own business for many years. In the capacity of my job here I have evaluated hundreds of businesses, but have never found one I would want to own, until I saw yours." I was shocked beyond words.

I explained the process and we went on to have many more conversations on the subject, but Mike became my second franchisee. He was (next to my own children being in the business) the most fantastic franchisee I could have been blessed to team with. Besides his great business ability, Mike and I shared many common areas. Both of our fathers were Pastors and we shared stories of our childhoods as "preacher's kids"—PKs. We had similar personality traits and there was instant rapport when we initially met. We just plain liked each other and became the best of friends. To this day, we are prayer warriors for each other in times of need.

Mike knuckled down, took the EA exam and also passed it on the first try. He started his Tax Tiger Franchise the year after John Paul, and today he has a very successful and thriving business. I am unspeakably proud of him and all he has accomplished.

Franchise #3

It took me two years to get the first two franchises, one per year. My goal was two per year, but God had other plans as always. I had lots of inquiries, and people flying in to take a look at what I had to offer, but either they weren't the right fit for me or they couldn't come up with the money to buy one. The economy still was impacting the availability of loans and financing. I have a pretty stringent set of values that I am looking for in a franchisee and few can measure up. Starting with:

- I am looking for people whose main goal is making a difference in people's lives (since that's my company core value) instead of the greed factor in the money that is to be made. Because this is a lucrative industry and there are so many taxpayers who need help, and there will never be a shortage of clients, most people go into this industry for purely that greed factor.

- In addition, I need business owners who have the same values of honesty and integrity, and a commitment to quality service that is my foundation with Tax Tiger. I have turned many away who, in my opinion, did not meet those qualifications.

My first year when I sent out an initial round of letters to companies, I received a response from a partner in a law firm in Little Rock, Arkansas, expressing some interest. Neil Deininger was one of three partners and was already in the tax resolution business and was very successful. He had a very successful law firm and did a large amount of bankruptcy work as well as work in other areas of the law. When he initially contacted me, we had several very long discussions and he felt like I was too narrow in my representation of clients. He wanted me to expand my focus if he was to be involved. I gave it some honest consideration, but I did not want to expand my focus. I was doing just fine without getting into more extensive work. He was passionate about this additional service and therefore he passed on the opportunity to have a franchise. I was sorry to lose him. He is an extremely intelligent and knowledgeable attorney who I highly respected.

I did not hear from Neil again for almost three years. One day, out of the clear blue, he called and said he had been talking to an attorney friend, a person who was also a friend of mine, and my name came up; he was told I was doing very well. It prompted him to call me. I was surprised to hear from him and even more surprised to hear him say that maybe he was a "little hasty" before, and was willing to start talking again. I was totally shocked. We had the best conversation that day and I invited him to fly out and meet me and look over my operation. We could then decide if it was doable for both of us.

He flew out a month or so later, and when I met Neil, I had an immediate and positive connection with him. He is so likable and down-to-earth. We spent the whole day discussing the company and showing him how we operated. By the end of the day, he commented that we had one of the most impressive companies he had ever seen. This was high praise from a man who had already been in this field for twenty or so years. He said he would need to send his other two partners back to see us in a few weeks in order that they would all be in agreement in going forward.

His other two partners, Reba Wingfield and Nic Corry came to visit and they are equally delightful people. Very smart, hardworking, and willing to look at new ideas. They loved what they saw, went back and they all decided that this was a great way for them to expand their business. All of their current business was local, and they wanted to start reaching out to get some of the national business. Plus the kind of work they did was not the kind of work Tax Tiger was doing. We did not specialize in bankruptcy nor do large tax court cases as they did. This would be a totally new arena for them. They believed that it was better to own a part of Tax Tiger than try to reinvent the wheel and do it themselves. Our family was growing.

The three of them set up another company to run the franchise and flew their staff out to Sacramento to get trained. As Tax Tiger, Arkansas, and now up and running, they are a fantastic addition to the team of tigers we are growing. They provide knowledge at a higher level and are a huge blessing to me. In addition they travel and speak at conferences. This gave me another centrally located franchise, exposure nationally with their travel and speaking, and a high level of expertise with their awesome team.

Franchise #4

Finally, after walking slowly for three years, God decided I could jog a little. This fourth year of my franchising program, I sold two franchises in the same year instead of just one.

Remember Mike, my number two franchise in San Diego? He called up one day to tell me his younger brother, Jon Call, had graduated from college a few years prior and had a good business mind, was currently in sales and marketing for a Christian company. He said he had been talking to Jon about Tax Tiger and as Jon had watched Mike's business do so well, he was also interested in obtaining one. He wanted to own his own business and was ready to learn what he needed to learn. Wow, God is so good!

Calling Jon, we had several discussions and I invited him to fly out to visit me. He came and we went over the program.

He needed to work on rounding up his money but he was excited about having an office of his own. Recently married, he had a lovely wife and was very likable, just like his brother. David and I felt he would be a great addition to our team.

Jon told me how he believed God was leading him to join us and his heart was definitely in the right place ... and he met all my requirements.

As I write this, Jon and his wife Kelly have completed training, Jon has passed his EA exam, and they have opened an office in St. Paul, Minnesota. I know he will do a fantastic job and rainbows are on the horizon for them. I thank God for them, their willingness to learn something new, and their desire to help people who are hurting.

Lastly, as this book goes to print, we have obtained our newest franchise baby tiger, one in Denver, Colorado. This franchise will be owned and operated by three lovely and very skilled women who were unhappy with the company they were with and wanted to do better by people. It's a little like my own story when I left Roni Deutch. Patty, Martina and Jessica will be trained this month and I know will be hugely successful in Denver. God is good!!!

So, this vision that God put in my heart one summer day in the forest on a tree stump, four years later is a reality and a hugely successful enterprise. I praise His *holy* name. His hands are on my business, both of them. I am humbled and grateful for every blessing and bit of favor He has bestowed on me, and I continue to pray to be in the center of His will. My desire continues to be to make a difference in people's lives and give God the honor and glory for it all.

9

State of the Union—Hear Me Strong!

A s I begin to sum it up, I want to relate one last critical and dangerous occurrence that cropped up on the horizon of our industry last year. It will remain one of the areas where I am most proud of my personal achievement.

I say this not with a prideful spirit, but a grateful heart to God for giving me the ability to deal with it and the skills necessary to initiate success.

I say dangerous because this situation had the ability to take down the entire industry of tax resolution in one "fell swoop" within a 45-day period of time. This was critical and shocking to say the least.

One day, I received a letter in the mail from Mark Guimond, a lobbyist in Washington DC. It outlined a new regulation the FTC (Federal Trade Commission) had passed and was about to put into action. The new law was designed and targeted toward the credit card settlement industry. This industry was fraught with dishonest companies who were "ripping off" the public, offering to settle their credit card debt for a portion of what was owed. Instead of settling, they were charging large sums of money to the client and basically walking away from representing them. The result: the "rip-off" companies got the client's money and the client got nothing—no settlement with the credit card companies which were weighing heavy on their breaking backs.

It was fraud on the consumer, and the FTC determined they would put new regulations in place which would essentially shut the vast majority of them down.

Working on this regulation for a couple of years, the FTC had held hearings on it as required by law, and formulated new policies. These policies basically said that no fees could be charged up front for this work, and fees, as well, could not be charged until the settlement was reached with the credit card companies. After the end results were achieved, the fee could be charged. This essentially meant that companies would be working for free for however long it took to resolve the liability. Few if any could sustain this kind of policy; no company can work without getting paid. I knew that Tax Tiger couldn't.

The letter I received from Mark Guimond stated that he had been involved in the discussions and development process of this new regulation from the beginning. He stated that he had just discovered at the very last minute, right before being placed into law, that the FTC had added a small phrase into the middle of the many pages of details that these new policies would also cover tax debt. Guimond immediately recognized that this would also put the entire tax resolution industry out of business because we would not be able to work without a fee paid in the beginning of a case. It would simply be impossible as we have CPA's, staff and overhead to pay monthly while we work through each case. The "Offer in Compromise" work (which is the settlement part of what we do) often takes up to a year or more to settle.

As I read this letter, I was shocked and horrified that this could happen right under our noses with no one even noticing. We, as the tax resolution industry, did not have our legal right to hearings or input of any kind as the credit card industry had been given. The letter sounded credible and stated he had sent this same letter out to the top tax resolution companies in the nation with a Better Business rating of C or above. It also stated we, as voices within the industry, had little time to act if we wanted to save our industry. Since he had specific knowledge of these new regulations and had been involved in them from the beginning, he knew the details. There was a phone number on the letter.

I immediately called one of my competitors with whom I was friendly and asked if he had received the same letter. He said he had and it was garbage and he had thrown it in the trash. I asked why he thought so. He said the guy was just out soliciting business and using scare tactics to get money out of all of us. He used some harsh language and said he was not interested in following up with Mark. I called another competitor who said it wasn't his problem.

Puzzled with their responses, I had to dig further. If the lobbyist was right, we were all in trouble and there was no way I was going to stick my head in the sand. I had too much at stake. Calling the number on the letter, I spoke directly with Mark. The conversation was very enlightening. He cited chapter and verse, telling me where I could find these regulations on line and showed me the new verbiage containing the words "tax debt."

I did my homework and found Mark's information to be accurate. The information was clearly stated on the Internet, and it scared me very badly. I had worked so hard to get to where I was, and now the whole company could go under in 45 days.

I asked him for a list of all the companies he had sent the letter to, volunteering to call each to sound the alarm.

I called my friends back and pleaded with them to at least call and talk to Mark and hear him out. I prayed with an urgency and fervor that God would somehow help me to sound the alarm and give me the courage to stand alone for us all if I had to. Now, let me say again, as I have already said, there are a lot of companies in the tax resolution industry that are just as bad as the credit card rip-off companies. And I know that's what the FTC was trying to address. They just didn't do it right; didn't have an understanding of the differences in the industries; and didn't know the good guys from the bad guys.

In my conversation with Mark, he advised that we immediately form a coalition of companies to fight this regulation; and yes, it would cost us a considerable amount of money. I had no issue with the cost because people deserve to get paid for what they do, and as the Bible tells us, "a workman is worthy of his hire." I knew if we could get enough companies to join together and split the cost, it would be doable. I called

Mark back and told him I had made another try for my friends to call him and hoped they would. Because time was of the essence, I encouraged him to call them first, even suggesting that he would get through this time. In the meantime, I asked him for a list of all the companies he had sent the letter to, volunteering to call each to sound the alarm. Over 100 names on his list were immediately forwarded to me.

The calling worked and I was able to get a few more owners involved. Mark had reached my two friends, had a long conversation with them, and made them realize the danger. Now, they were on board. Within a couple of weeks, we had formed a coalition of companies, with four founding members being the decision makers for the group. These four major firms were myself, my two friends and another Christian-based company.

We collected money to hire Mark as our lobbyist and to get started. Knowing that we had to separate ourselves and "tax resolution" from the rest of the others specially stated, we determined our argument consisted primarily of the fact that the new regulation referred to "unsecured debt" when it talked about credit card or tax debt, while in fact, all tax debt is "secured." This, combined with the fact that the FTC had violated our rights by not giving us hearings of any kind, was a brilliant strategy. Tax debt is secured by the government with a "lien" either written or silent.

Mark went to see Alison Brown, the lead attorney for the FTC and many other legislative contacts with whom he had relationships. He went to see IRS people, who maintained they had jurisdiction over tax professionals, not the FTC. There were already regulations in place to govern and discipline bad tax professionals through the Office of Professional

Responsibility at the IRS. It was a hard and intense fight for a few weeks. I bathed the issue in prayer daily and asked for God's intervention.

One morning when we were all waiting for the decision, I was on the phone with Mark, and all of a sudden he shouted, "We won, the ruling was just published. **They took the words, 'tax debt' out of the rules.**" I screamed at the top of my lungs. My whole office wondered what was happening. Mark and I were cheering and shouting. "Praise God, Praise God, Praise God," I kept saying over and over.

Our business was safe. We could continue to make a difference in many lives. God's hand was on my business! He had been an awesome partner throughout my life and once again, I felt His presence.

The FTC said they would come back around with hearings for us at a later time, so our coalition board then spent the next few months developing legislation that we would put on the shelf until needed. This legislation left nothing to chance and was designed to weed out the bad apples in our industry while not adversely impacting those of us who operate correctly and within the existing laws. This proposed legislation still sits on the shelf waiting to be brought out if they come after us again. Lastly, Mark advised recently that we form an actual association of tax resolution companies for our own protection. We did this in 2012 with a formal meeting in Washington, DC.

I feel proud and blessed to have played a major part in this end result, with all honor and glory going to my heavenly Father who continues to grant favor on my efforts. I have no doubt that the National Association of Tax Resolution Companies (NATRC) will continue to grow, and I'm honored that I was a founding member of the coalition.

Where Is Tax Tiger Today?

Tax Tiger continues to resolve many hundreds of client's tax issues and makes a huge difference in their financial lives. You can find a sampling of testimonials in the Appendix—testimonials that come from ordinary people who have encountered extraordinary financial situations, situations that are becoming all too common. We also have some high profile clients and a wide variety of many different professions who seek us out. Here is a recent example. The letter is from Annie Rodman, ex-wife of the basket ball professional, Dennis Rodman.

> After my divorce from Dennis, I found myself in the devastating situation of owing the IRS over one million dollars. It was my worst nightmare and there was no way I could afford to pay it. I searched for someone to help me and met with a tax attorney in Sacramento who told me he could help me for a fee of $100,000. There was no way I could afford that, and I left with a greater fear than I had before.

Then I called Tax Tiger and went in for a free consultation. I felt immediate peace as their office is calming and beautiful. Prior to this meeting, the IRS had levied my checking account and taken everything I had, even though I had signed an Installment Agreement. I had a baby to support and no money to buy food or pay the rent.

What a tremendous relief it was to meet Kathy Hill, who immediately put my mind at ease and explained the process of settling with the IRS. We filled out all the paperwork and Tax Tiger went to work. It was a very long process of over four years, fighting the IRS at every step.

Kathy instilled a sense of peace and comfort and the worry and fear faded. She and her team worked so hard and for so long that I was amazed there was such a company who would go the extra mile without ever asking for more money along the way. Four long years later, they settled with me for $11,000 and I was beyond ecstatic. Kathy never gave up on me or got tired of fighting them. Her tenacity is something to behold, and her company a blessing to all needing help. I give her the highest recommendation and praise for a job well done.

Annie Rodman

Since money and taxes owed is what brings clients to us, we continue to search for ways to increase our marketing presence for the lowest cost. We maintain the highest level of service possible and our rating at the Better Business Bureau continues to be an A+ as it has been for all of our years in business. David continues to run the operation well and remains one of God's greatest blessings to me. I have an awesome staff and a beautiful place to come to work each day. God is good! Everywhere I look, I can see His hand continues to be on my business.

The big three mega firms I mentioned in the beginning of this book and for whom I prayed for years that God would somehow take them all down so that they could no longer harm people, imploded in 2012. **All three in the same year!** It was astounding and unbelievable. News articles of these events are included in the Appendix.

- In August 2010, the State of California entered a $34 million dollar lawsuit against Roni Deutch, television's "Tax Lady," for orchestrating a "heartless scheme" that swindled thousands of people facing serious and expensive tax collection problems with the IRS. She subsequently closed her business after a receiver was appointed, surrendered her law license and is awaiting trial. (It took a couple of years of legal actions but by 2012 she was done.)

- *JK Harris* had charges filed against him by many state attorneys general and owes millions of dollars in lawsuits by them for taking fees and not performing the work. JK Harris was personally led away in handcuffs and forced into bankruptcy, effectively closing his business.

• *Tax Masters* had legal action filed against them this past year by the Texas Attorney General and has closed their company and filed for bankruptcy.

Wow! Hundreds of thousands of people who were ripped off by these companies now see them for what they really are, and the hundreds of thousands more who might have used them in the future have been spared financial loss.

Even though I prayed for it, this was overwhelming evidence of God's power and might to see Him bring down the top three multi-million dollar firms **all in one year**. And it wasn't soon enough!

Tax Tiger Franchising LLC is thriving and doing extremely well. Our franchises are all awesome and represent our values and principles extremely well and I love each one of them dearly. God will bring others to us as He sees fit in His plan to complete my vision of covering the nation with the best there is of the best. I'm grateful for what He has given me and pray for each office and their success and profitability daily. His hand continues to be on this business.

On a personal note, my marriage came to an end with a divorce in the fall of 2012. I moved out of the home four years earlier when an incident happened, and, as a result, God finally told me I could go. I stayed as long as I could; not wanting to compound one sin with another until He said it was time. Even then, I didn't file for divorce for four years and tried to keep a degree of friendship with Dick. Remember, he owned half of my business and California is a community property state. I was terrified that I would lose my business in a divorce that would require me to pay him half, which I didn't have any ability to do. I tried not to rock the boat and continued to pray for God's solution and support. This is another by-product of being unequally yoked together not only in marriage but in business. It is not His way.

One day, out of the blue, the answer came to me. The words flowed through me when I heard in prayer one early morning, "Buy him out, and then file for divorce." I sat down with a calculator and tried to devise a plan where I would/could offer to buy him out. I came up with an amount I believed was more than fair and proposed payments over time. Dick accepted it. A huge weight was lifted from my spirit.

To this day, I continue to pray for his salvation as I don't want to see him go to hell. I'm thankful for the good times we had and try to role model God's grace and mercy to him whenever I can. Beyond that, it's up to God. The business is now all mine, sink or swim—it's on me. But as my Lord walks with me daily, I will always swim.

I don't know what the future holds, but God laid on my heart in a clear and strong way this task, to write my story, the one that you have in your hands. I strongly believe He wants me to share with you the principles I have followed which draws His hand to hover over my businesses and the resulting favor I am blessed to experience.

I close with a scripture He put on my heart to share with you. It's Philippians 4:9 and reads,

Whatever you have learned or received or heard from me, or seen in me—*put it into practice*. And the God of peace will be with you. —NIV

Or from the King James Version,

Those things, which ye have both learned and received, and heard and seen in me, do: and the God of peace shall be with you.

Both the terms, "*put it into practice*" and "*do*" I want to leave you with, because if God has laid it on your heart to follow the components I have outlined in this book and are listed in the Appendix, and *if you desire God's hand on your business in a greater way*, then **DO it, bring Him in and embrace His words!**

Finally, I would be remiss if I did not close with the same question God asked me as I lay in bed one night at the age of 12. Where would you go if you died tonight? I have no way to know your heart or spiritual relationship with God, but should you have finished this book realizing that you haven't received Him into your heart as my Sunday School teacher did long ago, I invite you to accept Him now.

John 3:16 says,

For God so loved the world (that's you) that
He gave His one and only Son, that whoever
Believes in him shall not perish but have eternal life.

This means God gave His Son Jesus to die for you so you can have an eternal home in heaven with Him. All you have to do is simply believe.

Next, Romans 10:9-10 says,

That if you confess with your mouth, Jesus is Lord, and believe in your heart that God raised him from the dead, you will be saved. For it is with your heart that you believe and are justified, and it is with your mouth that you confess and are saved.

You need to pray a prayer to Jesus that says this:

"Lord Jesus, I need you. Thank you for dying on the cross for my sins. I open the door of my life and receive you as my Savior and Lord. Thank you for forgiving my sins and giving me eternal life. Make me the kind of person you want me to be."

If you pray this prayer, embrace it within your life and believe you will be saved, it will be so.

It is my deepest desire to all who read *Is God's Hand on your Business?* that first and foremost, you know the Lord as your personal Savior. And lastly that your business will experience the favor and blessings that mine has and that the Hand of God will rest over your business always.

May God richly bless your business and grant you favor beyond imagination.

Kathy

Appendix A

15 Essential Principles to Achieving Success and Prosperity

1. Desire and pray to be in the center of God's will daily
2. The power of prayer is mighty and awesome
3. Unwavering faith and trust; Faithfulness
4. Listening for God's words as He speaks to you
5. Be willing to learn new things
6. Be willing to do whatever it takes
7. Desire to continually draw closer to God
8. Give God constant praise and gratitude
9. Have Godly values
10. Daily morning Bible and devotional reading
11. Daily morning worship music
12. Regular and faithful church attendance
13. Tithe
14. Healthy office environment
15. Acknowledge and learn from mistakes

Appendix B

30 Key Scriptures to Inspire and Guide You

1. **Jeremiah 29:11**
    For I know the plans I have for you, declares the Lord, plans to prosper you and not to harm you; plans to give you hope and a future. (This is my personal favorite.)

2. **I Corinthians 2:9**
    However, as it is written: No eye has seen, no ear has heard, no mind has conceived what God has prepared for those who love Him.

3. **Proverbs 3:5-6**
    Trust in the Lord with all your heart and lean not on your own understanding; in all your ways acknowledge him and He will direct your paths.

4. **Philippians 4:6-7**
    Do not be anxious about anything, but in everything, by prayer and petition, with thanksgiving, present your requests to God. And the peace of God, which transcends all understanding, will guard your hearts and your minds in Christ Jesus.

5. **Psalm 37:4-5**
    Delight yourself in the Lord and He will give you the desires of your heart. Commit your way to the Lord; trust in him and He will do this.

6. **John 15:7-8**

   If you remain in me and my words remain in you, ask whatever you wish, and it will be given you. This is to my Father's glory, that you bear much fruit, showing yourselves to be my disciples.

7. **Proverbs 16:3**

   Commit to the Lord whatever you do, and your plans will succeed.

8. **Philippians 4:19**

   And my God will meet all your needs according to his glorious riches in Christ Jesus.

9. **Proverbs 11:25**

   A generous man will prosper ...

10. **Proverbs 20:24**

    A man's steps are directed by the Lord. How then can anyone understand his own way?

11. **Psalm 5:12**

    For surely, O Lord, you bless the righteous;
    you surround them with your favor as with a shield.

12. **Romans 8:28 and 31**

    And we know that in all things God works for the good of those who love him, who have been called according to his purpose. ...if God be for us, who can against us?

13. **Matthew 17:20**

    He replied, "Because you have so little faith. I tell you the truth, if you have faith as small as a mustard seed, you can say to this mountain, "move from here to there" and it will move. Nothing will be impossible for you.

14. **Proverbs 21:5**

    The plans of the diligent lead to profit as surely as haste lead to poverty.

15. **Mark 11:24**

    Therefore I tell you, whatever you ask for in prayer, believe that you have received it, and it will be yours.

16. **Joshua 1:8**

    Do not let this Book of the law depart from your mouth; meditate on it day and night, so that you may be careful to do everything written in it. Then you will be prosperous and successful.

17. **Malachi 3:8-10**

    Will a man rob God? Yet you rob me. But you ask, "How do we rob you?" In tithes and offerings ... bring the whole tithe into the storehouse, that there may be food in my house. "Test me in this", says the Lord Almighty, "and see if I will not throw open the floodgates of heaven and pour out so much blessing that you will not have room enough for it."

18. **Luke 6:38**

    Give and it will be given to you, A good measure, pressed down, shaken together and running over will be poured into your lap. For with the measure you use, it will be measured to you.

19. **II Corinthians 9:6**

    Remember this: Whoever sows sparingly will also reap sparingly, and whoever sows generously will also reap generously.

20. **Proverbs 21:21**
He who pursues righteousness and love finds life, prosperity, and honor.

21. **Psalm 1:2**
But his delight is in the law of the Lord, and on his law he meditates day and night.

22. **Proverbs 13:22**
... but a sinner's wealth is stored up for the righteous.

23. **Proverbs 15:77**
The greedy bring ruin to their households ...

24. **John 16:33**
I have told you these things, so that in me you may have peace. In this world you will have trouble. But take heart! I have overcome the world.

25. **Proverbs 10:22**
The blessing of the Lord brings wealth, and he adds no trouble to it.

26. **Psalm 69:30**
I will praise God's name in song and glorify him with thanksgiving.

27. **Psalm 37:23, 24**
If the Lord delights in a man's way, he makes his steps firm; though he stumble, he will not fall, for the Lord upholds him **with his hand**.

28. **Deuteronomy 8:18**
But remember the Lord your God, for it is he who gives you the ability to produce wealth, and so confirms his covenant, which he swore to your ancestors, as it is today.

29. **Psalm 60:5**

Save us and help us with **your right hand**, that those you love may be delivered.

30. **Psalm 63:8**

I will cling to you; your **right hand upholds me.**

Appendix C

Favorite Worship Songs

Song	Artist	Album
1. How Great is Our God	Chris Tomlin	Amazing Graze
2. Here I Am To Worship	Lenny LeBlanc	Songs 4 Worship Country
3. Awesome God	Michael Smith	Decades of Worship
4. Amazing Grace	Chris Tomlin	See The Morning
5. I Will Rise	Chris Tomlin	Hello Love
6. Amazing Love	Chris Rice	Open The Eyes of my Heart
7. Open The Eyes of My Heart	Phillips Craig and Dean	Let My Words Be Few
8. Mighty To Save	Hillsong	The I Heart Revolution
9. You Are My King	Newsong	More Life
10. They That Wait Upon the Lord	Stuart Hamblen	Gospel

Appendix D

Heart Letters from Jail

I have been a Prison Ministries volunteer for going on four years now and as such, have committed to a regular Tuesday evening Bible study in our main Sacramento jail. I teach the women on one of the floors in this jail. The blessings I have received from this commitment have far exceeded anything else I have ever done for the Lord. My objective is to lead them to the Lord and I never close a Bible study without offering God's plan of salvation to them. As a result, many have come to the Lord over the years. I go home rejoicing each and every time.

Those who already know the Lord have told me they have found their faith strengthened by my teaching. And many who have gotten out of jail have come to my church and sat in my row with me. The first time this happened, I couldn't hold back the tears.

Satan tries hard to keep me out of jail! He must stay up at night plotting ways for me to be unable to teach. There is only one room where all these women can gather for Bible Study and, on occasion, there will be an inmate who is violent or has threatened suicide; she will be held in that room for a period of time. When that happens, of course, the room is not available for me and my study group.

There have been too many such occasions where I have arrived at the jail only to find an inmate in that room and I had to return home without doing my study. That is Satan at work. Each Tuesday, therefore, I pray mightily, before I go, for God to bind Satan.

On one occasion, I had just started my study, opened my Bible, and started feeling dizzy. I carried on for a moment but realized that if I didn't lie down immediately, I was going to faint. I was sitting on a long table speaking to the women and so I just laid down on it. I didn't know what else to do and I was quite embarrassed. The reaction among the women in the group was amazing! They jumped up and started praying out loud for me, asking God to protect me. The correctional officers reacted quickly; they entered the room, made all the women return to their cells and the medics appeared and took me down to the clinic.

After a few minutes, I recovered and was able to drive home. It turned out to be the onset of food poisoning, and I was sick for the next two days. Satan stopped my study "cold" that night. Fortunately, these times are few and far between; greater is He that is in me than he that is in the world.

These women eagerly look forward to my study each time and often write letters that are very meaningful to me. I have included five of them for you to read:

What do I get from Ms. Kathy's
Bible Study?

I get a wonderful living example of
God's Love. When she talks, I feel the
power and strength of the Holy Spirit. I
get goosebumps when we pray and when
she hugs me. I've never before wanted
to read the Bible and learn it's teachings.
Now, because of her, I hunger for the
word and the knowledge I'm learning.
I look forward each Tuesday, that I
know she will be here, to hearing her
teachings and feeling the Love she makes
sure to share with all of us. I am
grateful for the time she spends with
us and feel blessed to know her.

Thanks Ms. Kathy for ALL you do.

MICHELE

Miss Kathy, I want to writ- you what you/your Bible studies mean to us, for you for Christmas! So here goes to me: You and your Bible study mean the world to me! This is the darkest, most scary, helpless, and hopeless I've ever felt in my life! My Grandma who helped raise me passed away, 4-13-12 and then Lucus got himself shot to death, 5-18-12 when I came here! I hated sacramento and felt so beyond alone and scared! One day I got up to get out of my cell and get a Bible and I met you! Your joy and great love for God and Jesus radiates off you something fierce, I couldn't help but see and feel it right through my tears, fear and pain! You reached me and brought me back into the light! And you keep doing it every-time I see you! This is why you and your Bible study mean the world to me! Thank you for being you Miss Kathy, an angel in my life! God bless you and yours!

♡ les

Leslie

What you being here means to me.

   It means that even though ive made mistakes im still important. That im not just a last name or number. That somebody still believes theres a worthy person. You leaving your family on Christmas night to come be with us ment so much to me i dont even know how to put it into words. You are truely one of gods angels and he has a very special place for you right next to him. Not a single person in my family or husband or in laws nobody even put money on there phone for me to call or came to visit an all my family lives here in Soe. Thank you sooo much

♡

Barrios

  "What does Miss Kathys Bible Study Mean To Me.....
  "I go to 3 Bible Studies a week and yours by far takes the cake⌣!:"I learn so much just by the way God speaks thru you! I Look forward to your humble Spirit every other week! I wish you could come daily! I Love the way you treat us as equals, and how you remind us everytime you come how we are forgiven I Love You Miss Kathy! Thank God For you!

MRS. Kathy

What I got from the Stone of
Joseph is that no matter
what Jesus never gave Him
anything He couldn't Handle
and He never Lost His faith.

Mrs Kathy I enjoy you so much
when you come to spend time
with us your beautiful heart
Just shines so bright I Just
want to thank you for being
you God Bless you
                              Amen

        Jennifer

Appendix E

Seven Key Tax Tiger Testimonials

It was hard to select just seven from the hundreds we received. But these few letters will let you read and experience the tremendous calling that God has led me to, in helping these hurting people and making such a difference in their lives. I never tire of this calling and have loved every minute of it from day one. May God continue to use my company and all my franchises for this very reason.

. . .

Testimonial Letter 1:

A True Story—

I have tears rolling down my face as I begin to share my story with you. It is very hard for me to write about my shameful life and how I was about to take my own life. I'm writing this in hopes that I can in my own way help someone in need as I was helped by Tax Tiger and my ex-wife.

The time goes by so fast, it seems like it was just a couple of years ago that I was a little boy growing up in East L.A. There was a lot of violence in my neighborhood and in my home; as a result I started drinking at the age of 12. I didn't have any guidance from my mother and my father left the house when I was eight years old.

At the age of 19 I got married and my wife did our taxes and paid our bills. After our divorce I started drinking heavily again and went from job to job and ended up homeless. After going from state to state and homeless, I met my last wife. We fell in love, got married and divorced all in a year and a half due to my drinking. I ended up in Florida in 2009 and continued living a nightmare of a life. My brother heard that I was in Florida and not doing too well, so he came to check on my safety. I was very glad to see him; I had not seen him in years. He stayed with me in my little trailer and the next day we went out on a boat ride with my neighbor and his new boat. My brother decided he wanted to go for a swim and jumped in the water; he started having problems and went down. My neighbor and I jumped in to save him, they both went down and didn't come up. They both drowned right in front of me!

I was in shock and numb at the same time. I walked around in a daze. A couple of months later I went to the bank to get what little money I had to buy food and something to drink. The IRS levied my bank account. THAT WAS IT! I could not do this anymore. I could not live like this anymore! I went and got a gun and called my ex-wife to say I was sorry for all the problems I caused her and I was going to kill myself.

She pleaded and begged me not to do it and to give her two hours. She said that she would help by giving me some money for food and would find someone that would help me with the IRS. About 20 minutes later she called me back and gave me two phone numbers. I called the first one; it was Tax Tiger, I talked to one of their excellent financial analysts and told him I was ready to leave this world but I promised my ex-wife I would make ONE phone call. He talked to me for a very long time. He prayed for me and assured me that he was going to help. He made me give him my word that I would not do anything stupid until he was about to help me. My case was assigned to an awesome professional enrolled agent (A GREAT MAN). He worked on my case for a year and a half. I had a lot of homework and many hours of paper work for months at a time. It was not easy and I wanted to quit many times, but I gave my word to both of them as well as my ex-wife that I would not quit! This gave me new hope for my life and maybe get back with my ex-wife, but this was not meant to be. On May 23, 2012 the IRS accepted our offer in compromise of $129,629.00 for ONLY $50.00!

I WANT TO THANK KATHY HILL (CEO) AND HER AWESOME AND PROFESSIONAL STAFF (I WOULD NOT BE HERE IF IT WASN'T FOR THEM) AND MY EX-WIFE FOR LOVING ME UNCONDITIONALLY!

I HAVE NOT DRANK SINCE!

• • •

Testimonial Letter 2:

To Whom It May Concern,

First and foremost, I offer up praise and honor to God for the blessings He has bestowed upon my life. Next, I would like to express my deepest appreciation and gratitude to Kathy Hill and the Tax Tiger staff for the professional, courteous service I received in resolving my IRS and FTB liabilities.

My experience with Kathy Hill and Tax Tiger was without doubt a divinely inspired appointment. As a recently reborn Christian dealing with consequences of poor "worldly" choices—not the least of which included a monumental federal and state tax liability—I never would have found Tax Tiger if I hadn't heard their advertisement on my local Christian radio station, and obeyed the prompting of the Holy Spirit to call them.

Honestly, I believed my situation was hopeless, I was embarrassed to admit my circumstances to a "snooty" attorney that I wouldn't be able to afford. To my amazement, Kathy was willing to take my case. The entire staff treated me with dignity and respect. And despite having only disability income, an affordable payment plan was established.

Kathy is truly anointed in her profession. She negotiated an IRS Offer in Compromise reducing my liability of $19,706.00 to $210.00. As if that wasn't miraculous enough, she also took on the state Franchise Tax Board and my liability of $5,115.30 was totally written off! I am so blessed to be given a clean slate and a fresh start in life!

I strongly recommended to anyone facing similar circumstances please do not delay in retaining Tax Tiger to assist you with your tax problems. The IRS and state tax collectors are ruthless, and Tax Tiger is a formidable advocate on your behalf. I will definitely continue to retain Tax Tiger to handle all my future tax returns.

• • •

Testimonial Letter 3:

Dear Kathy & Tax Tiger Staff,

I want to express our thanks to you for standing by us throughout the past year. I believe it was of no coincidence that I happened upon your website a year and half ago. That very same morning I had mentioned to the Lord when I was in prayer for help in the matter of our tax debt. Later that day I was surfing the web for the irs.gov site; only I miss-typed the address and came across many different sites that offered similar help as yours. For some reason your site stood out and after I read just about all the info you provided I decided it was worth looking into. Since then, I can't say it was all downhill from there, but through some more ups and downs as trials go, over the past year, Kathy and Tax Tiger stood right by us, fighting our case with a Victory in the end!!! You have incredible integrity and the very fact that you are faith believers was a very big plus in my opinion. Not every company out there walks the talk and talks the walk, but Tax Tiger does.

We have had this tax debt hanging over our head for the last 13 years, when my husband first became self-employed. We were living on what we earned and could not pay our taxes, and every year it just kept increasing. By the time we sought help we owed $18,946 but, when Kathy and Tax Tiger were finished with everything they decreased that amount by more than half of what we owed. It feels like we can breathe for the first time again in a long time. Also, it won't be long and our offer in compromise will be settled in full. Believe me; I will really be doing a dance when that day arrives.

Thank you, Thank you, so much everyone at Tax Tiger for helping us out of a deep pit of debt. WE will not forget what you have done for us. We could not have done it without God and you on our side!

God Bless You All!

Sincerely,

• • •

Testimonial Letter 4:

My name is Kimberly, and after being married for almost three years to a man who physically and mentally abused me ... I finally escaped him and spent another year hiding from him with my then 13-year-old daughter. When I finally started feeling like I didn't need to look over my shoulder any longer, I discovered that in all the time I had been with this person and he had been informing me that our taxes had been being taken care of by a family member of his that was an accountant that in reality he had done nothing. At this time I realized I was six years behind in back taxes ... once again, I was living in horror not knowing where to turn.

I went online one day searching for help and discovered a Christian organization by the name of Tax Tiger. I called them immediately and by the time I got off the phone with them, I felt I had had a ton of bricks removed from my shoulders. The next few months they stayed in constant contact with me and any time I had questions they were always very considerate and helpful.

Tax Tiger helped me tremendously and after going back and forth with the IRS for me, they reached an agreement and a Settlement with the IRS.

What could have been many years of trying to pay back what I owed in back taxes turned out to be only five months. I just mailed off my last payment to the IRS last week and feel such pride and relief that I took the step forward to take care of this obligation. Without Tax Tiger and the wonderful group of people that work there, I would probably still be living my life looking over my shoulder ... instead I'm holding my head high.

Thank you so very much, Tax Tiger, and you know who I'm referring to. Each of you who worked my case. God Bless You and Keep You Safe.

• • •

Testimonial Letter 5:

Dear Kathy and Tax Tiger Staff,

I am writing to say THANK YOU, THANK YOU from the bottom of my heart. I found the Tax Tiger website in the middle of an anxious night when things were closing in on me and I was confused about what to do. I know it was Divine since I couldn't tell you how I got to your website. It was meant to be. I called the next day and received concrete information to begin to set my course for clearing many years of avoiding an ever-growing problem. I was so relieved that I was NOT in this alone. Kathy and her staff are reassuring, comforting and help you EVERY STEP of the way. There is just not enough great things to describe TAX TIGER. Kathy is the leader of a professional, no-nonsense, get-the-job-done company. She will offer you a way out that is reasonable in price, while reassuring the problem will be resolved in the biggest way possible. I am one of their best advertisements.

I had to file nine years of back "procrastination" to IRS and came out owing a huge amount. The settlement was incredible and doable. If you are looking for a SUPERIOR company with an A plus customer service, you have now FOUND IT IN TAX TIGER. Kathy, you truly are doing a terrific service for folks like me. Thanks AGAIN.

• • •

Testimonial Letter 6:

Dear Kathy Hill and Associates,

First and foremost, I thank our Lord and Savior Jesus Christ, by a miracle I found Tax Tiger in the phone book advertising your Christian belief and helping people with their tax problems. We are relieved, blessed and thankful that this long and frustrating endeavor is finished. You kept your word and through your expertise we are thrilled and so thankful that this settlement is over. God bless!!!

Testimonial Letter 7:

From a client, Annie Rodman, ex-wife of the basketball professional, Dennis Rodman—

After my divorce from Dennis, I found myself in the devastating situation of owing the IRS over one million dollars. It was my worst nightmare and there was no way I could afford to pay it. I searched for someone to help me and met with a tax attorney in Sacramento who told me he could help me for a fee of $100,000. There was no way I could afford that, and I left with a greater fear than I had before.

Then I called Tax Tiger and went in for a free consultation. I felt immediate peace as their office is calming and beautiful. Prior to this meeting, the IRS had levied my checking account and taken everything I had, even though I had signed an Installment Agreeement. I had a baby to support and no money to buy food or pay the rent.

What a tremendous relief it was to meet Kathy Hill, who immediately put my mind at ease and explained the process of settling with the IRS. We filled out all the paperwork and Tax Tiger went to work. It was a very long process of over four years, fighting the IRS at every step.

Kathy instilled a sense of peace and comfort and the worry and fear faded. She and her team worked so hard and for so long that I was amazed there was such a company who would go the extra mile without ever asking for more money along the way. Four long years later, they settled with me for $11,000 and I was beyond ecstatic. Kathy never gave up on me or got tired of fighting them. Her tenacity is something to behold and her company a blessing to all needing help. I give her the highest recommendation and praise for a job well done.

Annie Rodman

Appendix F

News Clippings from Tax Predators

THE SACRAMENTO BEE
Published: Sunday, Apr. 21, 2013 - 12:00 am | Page 1D

Personal Finance: When tax 'help' is just a mirage

By Claudia Buck
cbuck@sacbee.com

Maria Garcia never dreamed she would land in so much trouble with the IRS. But a few years ago, she found herself owing about $32,000 in back taxes—a situation she says was partly caused by a family member fraudulently using her name and Social Security number for work.

Desperate for help, Garcia turned to TaxMasters, one of the many "tax relief" companies advertising heavily on TV, radio and the Internet.

"I'd run into tax problems, and their advertising was enticing," said the Roseville resident and mother of four adult children. "Needless to say, it was a fiasco. They prey on your fears of the IRS coming and taking what little you have: my car, my wages. ..."

After paying about $4,000 in upfront fees—and giving the company power of attorney to represent her before the Internal Revenue Service—Garcia thought her problems were over. Instead, they just got worse.

Months went by without any resolution. Meanwhile, the IRS tax penalties and interest kept climbing. After a year or so, Garcia owed more than $42,000.

"Every time I emailed (TaxMasters), they said: 'We're working on it.'"

In March 2012, the company, Texas-based TaxMasters Inc., filed for bankruptcy, leaving thousands of hapless taxpayers, including Garcia, in worse shape than when they started.

Every year, as the tax season closes, many Americans are unable to pay their full IRS bill or resolve their past-due obligations. These folks are often the target of "tax relief" companies.

As the economy perks up, many of these companies actually drum up more business, said Gary Almond, president of the Northeast California Better Business Bureau. "As the economy improves, some (consumers) want to resolve their past debts. They now may have equity in their home to resolve debt. Or they want to refinance their mortgage and need to settle their tax liens. Or they've become employed again and find that their wages are being garnished."

While plenty of legitimate companies offer tax help to struggling consumers, a number of unethical companies, especially those charging high upfront fees, prey on unsuspecting taxpayers.

On its website, the Federal Trade Commission warns against companies charging upfront fees while claiming they can "reduce or even eliminate" tax debts.

"The truth is that most taxpayers don't qualify for the programs these fraudsters hawk, their companies don't settle the tax debt, and in many cases don't even send the necessary paperwork to the IRS," notes the FTC's website.

In all cases, consumers should be wary of too-good-to-be-true claims.

"Some of these 'effectiveness' claims should be taken with a grain of salt. Everyone's case is different; there are no blanket guarantees," said the BBB's Almond.

In California, state Franchise Tax Board officials say free help is available, particularly for those facing financial hardships.

"Taxpayers seeking help should be aware that the same debt relief options are available, regardless if (they) use a 'tax relief' company or handle it on their own," FTB spokesman Daniel Tahara said in an email.

"When a taxpayer can't pay, we prefer to work with them to resolve the collection issue … as quickly as possible through the method best suited for their situation." (See box for details on IRS and FTB repayment options.)

Among the more notorious tax-resolution empires was run by former Sacramento attorney Roni Deutch, who famously branded herself "The Tax Lady" in late-night cable TV ads. Starting from a solo law practice in the late 1990s, Deutch eventually presided over a $25 million-a-year company with franchises and offices in 23 states.

In 2010, then-state Attorney General Jerry Brown filed a lawsuit accusing Deutch of swindling thousands of customers facing IRS tax woes. The state's lawsuit said she charged individual clients up to $4,700 for tax help but delivered little or no results. As part of the lawsuit, she was ordered to pay $435 million in refunds to unsatisfied clients.

———

Defiantly maintaining her innocence, Deutch eventually closed her offices and surrendered her law license in May 2011, saying she was broke and unable to keep her company going.

While companies like Deutch's and TaxMaster have been magnets for complaints, other tax-relief firms operate virtually complaint free.

"There are so many bad ones, but the credible companies are making a difference in people's lives," said Kathy Hill, founder and CEO of Tax Tiger in Sacramento, a tax resolution company with franchises in three other states.

Last year, she and others formed the National Association of Tax Resolution Companies, a Washington, D.C.-based group whose mission is to preserve the industry's reputation and protect consumers from "unfair and deceptive" tax-resolution advertising tactics.

"It's an association of the 'good guys,'" says Hill, whose firm has an A-plus rating from the BBB.

With first-time clients, Hill's company typically does a free financial consultation, looking at income, assets and monthly expenses to see what kind of repayment plan is possible.

"If they have little to no assets—no equity in a home, no 401(k), no investments, cars or real estate, they probably qualify for an 'offer in compromise,'" she said. A so-called OIC is where the IRS or Franchise Tax Board agrees to settle a tax debt for less than what is owed.

"The IRS hates the program because they have to settle for less than what's owed," said Hill. "But it's a blessing for those who can't pay the $50,000 or $60,000 they owe."

But it's not a quick-fix solution. Hill said it can take up to a year to get all the documentation and paperwork—everything from rental receipts to wages to car payments—submitted and approved by the IRS.

She typically charges a flat fee, anywhere from $1,000 to negotiate an IRS or FTB installment plan to $4,800 for more time-consuming offer-in-compromise settlements. Rather than an upfront fee, clients make an initial down payment, then pay the rest within 10 to 12 months.

One Tax Tiger customer, Roseville resident Jennifer Dunn, discovered a year or so ago that she was on the hook for nearly $70,000 owed to the IRS by her estranged husband's concrete business. Amid her divorce, "I tried resolving it on my own with the IRS but wasn't getting anywhere," said Dunn, who said the IRS payment plan was more than she could afford on her schoolteacher salary.

She turned to Hill, who arranged an IRS compromise settlement of $871. As part of the 2012 agreement, Dunn must file her taxes on time for the next six years, or the deal is off.

Dunn said the relief of resolving her situation is huge. "She (Hill) was a savior, I tell you."

To avoid getting defrauded by an unsavory company, do your homework, say state and local officials. Check with the Better Business Bureau or appropriate state agency for a company's record.

"With anybody who requires an upfront fee for a service they can't guarantee, run," said Mark Leyes, spokesman for the state Department of Corporations.

Currently, the IRS and its Taxpayer Advocate Service are working to resolve tax debts of former TaxMasters clients such as Maria Garcia.

Garcia, who works full time at a warehouse store, says she now wishes she had gone directly to the IRS for help. Her recent 2012 tax refund—$300—went straight to the IRS for repayment.

Looking back, "I made mistakes," Garcia said. "I thought I could fix it on my own. And I couldn't."

NEED TAX RELIEF? HERE'S HOW TO GET IT

INTERNAL REVENUE SERVICE

Under its "Fresh Start" program, delinquent taxpayers can request installment payments or an "offer-in-compromise" plan to wipe out existing tax debts. The IRS expanded its program in 2010, making it easier for more people to qualify.

Installment payments are generally available for individuals with up to $50,000 to repay. If approved, you repay in regular monthly payments, starting as low as $25.

For OICs, taxpayers must show they have no way of repaying their debt in a reasonable amount of time, based on their income and assets. In most cases, the tax debt must be $50,000 or less. Taxpayers offer a settlement amount, which is reviewed by the IRS.

The IRS has also raised the debt amount—to $10,000—that triggers a lien for unpaid back taxes being placed on a person's home or property.

For details on resolving IRS debts, go to: www.irs.gov. Or call (800) 829-1040 (individuals) or (800) 829-4933 (businesses).

FRANCHISE TAX BOARD

The FTB also offers installment-payment and offer-in-compromise plans for struggling taxpayers.

If the balance owed is up to $25,000 and can be paid within 60 months, the FTB has a simplified process for taxpayers to set up a monthly payment plan. For larger amounts, the process requires more documentation. Tax liens are not typically filed against taxpayers using payment plans.

For an offer-in-compromise, the FTB reviews the taxpayer's income and assets to determine if a compromise offer is acceptable. It can take 90 days or more to complete a review.

HELP FROM PROS

If you don't want to seek IRS or FTB relief alone, get help from professionals: CPAs, tax preparers, enrolled agents or reputable tax-resolution companies.

Before hiring anyone, check a company or individual's reputation with the Better Business Bureau or appropriate state or federal agencies.

Call The Bee's Claudia Buck, (916) 321-1968. Read her Personal Finance blog, www.sacbee.com/personalfinanceblog.

Reflections

As I reflect back on the landscape of my life and the last 20 years of business success that I have been blessed with, I marvel in awe and humility at the wondrous grace and mercy of God.

It's been an incredible journey, filled with many beautiful lakes, rivers, streams and mountain tops of joy and blessings. But the journey also had valleys, barren fields, and many bumps in the road along the way. Often the bumps were painful and filled with the tears of distress and hurt. Those were teaching events and lessons that needed to be learned and which ultimately worked out for the good for me. God's grace and mercy were always there and He never left me. He forgave on the occasions when I messed up and stood me back on my feet when I fell. At times he carried me, leaving only one set of footprints on the sand.

I want you to know, as you have now read through this amazing story of God's hand on my life, that you are not alone in facing the trials and tribulations of business success, or even in your personal life, for that matter. Never forget that as a child of God, He wants the very best for you. He has a master plan for your life and a plan for your business. He walks with you and guides you and if you will but listen carefully for His voice, follow His principles, read His words regularly and often, favor is yours.

The 15 Essential Principles to Achieve Success and Prosperity, I outlined in the book and listed in Appendix A, were given to me at various times in my Christian walk with Him and each one took me to a new level of closeness with Him. They may seem simple and some of them you have probably heard many times before. But until they become a regular and crucial part of your relationship with Him, that closeness you desire will fall short. The ultimate goal is to be as close to the Lord as you can possibly get in your relationship with Him. Because only in this quest for closeness can you experience the business and personal success you dream of and work for and begin to feel His favor in a mighty way.

We all make choices in life that affect our relationship with Him. I want you to be encouraged and feel supported as you make every effort to make the right choices and when you make a wrong one, remember that He will be there still.

It has been my honor and gift to share these simple truths with you. I desire to be used by Him to help you experience success and financial prosperity. I give Him all the glory, honor and praise. I know that if He can take a simple Tupperware lady and make her into a very successful CEO of two companies, He can take you and give you the favor you seek and let you feel His hand on your business like never before.

He has also laid it on my heart to give a limited number of personal seminars on these areas so look for one in your area coming soon. I would love to meet you.

In His name,

Kathy

About the Author

Kathy Hill grew up as a pastor's kid spending time in Colorado and California. She worked her way through business as a successful home-based Tupperware® lady to the CEO and founder of a national tax resolution company, Tax Tiger™, and along the way she inspired, motivated, and produced incredible results.

Her story is balanced with her unwavering faith in God, and what His place in your growing business should be. Trial after trial, success after success, nothing seemed to stand in the way of a business backed by God, nor would it stop that train from moving forward. After reading *Is God's Hand On Your Business?* you will most certainly envision a new outlook on your business today, and what the future should hold.

Some of the most successful CEOs and companies alike are headed by individuals with strong and unwavering faith, morals, ethics, and care for others. This book will take you on my journey, and hopefully inspire you.

How to Work with Tax Tiger

If you or someone you know has an IRS problem and needs help, Tax Tiger provides a free consultation and advises you of all your options. This is invaluable and informative. To receive your free consultation, call 1-866-667-3829.

Tax Tiger has offices in:

Austin, Texas

Carlsbad (San Diego), California

Littlerock, Arkansas

St. Paul, Minnesota

Denver, Colorado

We invite you to take advantage of our many years of experience and our stellar A+ reputation with the Better Business Bureau. For more information and a look at our success stories and testimonials, visit our website at:

www.TaxTiger.com

How to Bring Kathy to Your Organization

Kathy will be doing a limited number of one day seminars on her **15 Essential Principles of Success and Prosperity** which will be fun, entertaining and extremely informative. You will see a difference in your business and/or life after attending one of these life-altering seminars.

Her amazing story when heard in person is one that inspires and motivates a closer relationship with your heavenly Father.

She will also do speaking engagements to groups upon advance request.

Should you desire to enhance your life and financial goals, and bring Kathy to your organization, please contact her at:

www.KathyHillAuthor.com